Effective Practices for Dynamic Youth Ministry

D1367118

Effective Practices for Dynamic Youth Ministry

Thomas East
with
Ann Marie Eckert
Dennis Kurtz
Brian Singer-Towns

saint mary's press

The publishing team included Brian Singer-Towns, development editor; Kimberly Sonnek, cover designer; Andy Palmer, design coordinator; manufacturing coordinated by the production services department of Saint Mary's Press.

Produced with the assistance of D & G Limited, LLC. Project staff included: David Spiech, D & G Limited, LLC, copy editor; Stephanie Seifert, D & G Limited, LLC, production editor; D & G Limited, LLC, typesetter.

Printed in the United States of America

3397

ISBN 978-0-88489-806-1

Library of Congress Cataloging-in-Publication Data

East, Thomas (Thomas Joseph)
  Effective practices for dynamic youth ministry / Thomas East, with Ann Marie Eckert, Dennis Kurtz, Brian Singer-Towns.
      p. cm.
  ISBN 978-0-88489-806-1 (pbk.)
  1. Church work with youth. I. Eckert, Ann Marie. II. Kurtz, Dennis.
III. Singer-Towns, Brian. IV. Title.
  BV4447.E327 2004
  259'.23—dc22
                                                              2003025697

Authors' Acknowledgments

We wish to thank the following people for their support and assistance in the *Effective Youth Ministry Practices in Catholic Parishes* project:

- The youth, adult youth ministry leaders, and parish staff members who participated in the interviews. Your enthusiasm was contagious and your wisdom was inspiring.

- The diocesan leaders at each interview site who identified and invited the research participants and arranged the necessary details for the interviews. Without your generosity this project would never have happened.

- The symposium participants who discussed and reflected on the significance of our early research findings. Your insights helped us uncover what was truly significant.

- The effective practices leadership team. You set this project in the right direction with your honest feedback and generous support.

- Our research consultants Pamela Maykut and Richard (Mort) Morehouse. Without your guidance, encouragement, and friendship we would still be lost in an ocean of data.

This book is a summary report from the Effective Youth Ministry Practices in Catholic Parishes Project, which is sponsored by the Center for Ministry Development and Saint Mary's Press, in collaboration with the National Federation for Catholic Youth Ministry.

Funding for this project has been provided through the sponsoring agencies and the Louisville Institute, an anonymous Catholic foundation, and the Catholic Youth Foundation, USA.

Research Consultants
Richard (Mort) Morehouse, PhD, and Pamela Maykut, PhD, of Viterbo University served as consultants for this project.

Executive Committee and Research Team
Project Coordinator:
Thomas East, Director
Center for Ministry Development

Laurie Delgatto, Development Editor
Saint Mary's Press

Ann Marie Eckert, Project Coordinator for Youth Ministry Services
Center for Ministry Development

Pamela Johnson, Director of Services
Saint Mary's Press

Dennis Kurtz, Chair for the Youth Ministry Development Management Committee of the NFCYM

Mike Moseley, Project Coordinator for Youth Ministry Services
Center for Ministry Development

Brian Singer-Towns, Development Editor
Saint Mary's Press

Leadership Team
The Leadership Team for this project includes the Executive Committee listed above and the following individuals and organizations that provided collaborative support and consultation for the project:

Joanne Cahoon, Coordinator of Adolescent Catechesis
Archdiocese of Baltimore

Stan Cordero, Office of Religious Education and Youth Ministry
Archdiocese of San Francisco

Ken Johnson-Mondragón, MA, Programs Associate
Instituto Fe y Vida

Robert McCarty, Executive Director
National Federation for Catholic Youth Ministry

Barbara Anderson, Secretariat for Laity, Family, Women and Youth
USCCB

Dan Mulhall, Representative for Catechesis/Multicultural Concerns
Department of Education/USCCB

Lee Nagel, Director of Total Catholic Education
Diocese of Green Bay
Representative to the NCCL

Howard Roberts, Vice-Chairperson
National African American Catholic Youth Ministry Network

Anna Scally, President
Cornerstone Media

Cheryl Tholcke, Coordinator for Youth Ministry Services
Center for Ministry Development

Contents

Introduction

The world is filled with patterns. We can learn from these patterns if we stand back, see the connections, and listen to what they can teach us. This was the quest of the research team in the *Effective Youth Ministry Practices in Catholic Parishes* project, which was conducted by the Center for Ministry Development and Saint Mary's Press, in collaboration with the National Federation for Catholic Youth Ministry. These leaders in Catholic youth ministry sought to listen to youth and youth leaders in parishes with effective youth ministry so that youth may be better served in all Catholic parishes.

Catholic youth ministry has experienced tremendous growth through the work of dedicated and resourceful leaders who keep imagining and creating new ways for youth to be served and included in parishes. In 1997, the Catholic bishops of the United States approved *Renewing the Vision: A Framework for Catholic Youth Ministry* (RTV) as their blueprint for the continued development of effective youth ministry. Since then many parishes across the nation have developed dynamic ministry that implements the goals and components of this vision. Many more struggle. They want to know where to start or how to grow and enhance their youth ministry. It was with these communities in mind that the project partners pursued their aim to identify the practices of parishes with effective youth ministry.

Practices of Effective Youth Ministry

This research builds upon and complements other research in Catholic youth ministry by focusing on the practices of effective youth ministry. Practices are actions by an individual or a community in which values and beliefs are embedded. To discover what a family is, we see how they practice being a family—not just what they say they believe or just what they do, but the practices of how they are a family.

In a similar way, this project identified the practices of Catholic parishes that are effective in youth ministry. What are they doing when they are

I think youth ministry helps . . . the young people have a greater relationship with God. It makes them stronger in their lives as Christians and to just be able to grow to be very mature, healthy people.

Parish Staff

Effective youth ministry unleashes the power of youth faith witness to help young people grow in their own faith and to touch the hearts of peers and the entire faith community. Youth faith witness is vulnerable, bold, eloquent, deep, profound, authentic, vibrant, and moving. It includes, uplifts and invites.

Parish Staff

Across the board, in a number of programs in our parish, the youth are not only involved in leadership roles, but we have young catechists and . . . programs that are virtually run day by day by young people themselves."

Parish Staff

Research Findings

Common qualities, actions, and attitudes were present in parishes with dynamic youth ministry. These factors worked in concert to promote the transforming outcomes described. In addition to this overall finding about the transforming effect of youth ministry, twenty-three additional findings emerged from analysis of the interviews with youth, adults, and the parish staff members and are outlined in the chapters that follow. The appendices provide more information about the research project: Appendix A describes the process used in identifying the findings; Appendix B includes the twelve key findings for each group—youth, adult leaders, and parish staff members.

Each of the coming chapters identifies key findings; provides quotations from youth, adult youth ministry leaders and parish staff; and provides implications and recommendations that will help parishes take on these practices of effective youth ministry. Chapter 1 has five key findings on parish support for youth ministry. These findings describe the overall relationship of youth within the community, including the community's affection for youth and understanding of youth ministry. Chapter 2 has five overall findings that describe the qualities of ministry to youth in parishes with effective youth ministry. These findings name the life of youth as the starting point for ministry and describe innovation and responsiveness as the process for dynamic ministry.

Chapter 3 describes five high-impact program elements in effective youth ministry. Chapter 4 has five findings that describe the importance of leadership in effective youth ministry. Chapter 5 summarizes recommendations for parishes and provides additional insights about parishes with effective youth ministry practices.

Reading This Book

Parishes that are willing have effective practices of youth ministry. These communities know youth and because of their care and concern for young people, they include youth and respond to their needs in innovative and dynamic ways. The practice of youth ministry that was described by the parishes that took part in the research is relational and organic. If we know youth, we grow to care for them and desire to respond effectively to their needs and to include their incredible gifts. The practices of simple caring are found in most communities. In the parishes that participated in the research, these caring practices became the community's norms.

Reading this book is a sign that you care about youth and want to enhance youth ministry in a community. No matter what role you have in making youth ministry happen, your involvement and advocacy can help name ways for your community to grow. As you read about these parish communities, you are likely to identify with some practices and feel challenged by others. Look for these affirmations and challenges as you journey with these communities. They will help you name your starting point and, hopefully, lead the way to more dynamic and effective practices.

## CHAPTER 1

Parish Support for Youth Ministry

There is something special about the relationship between the overall parish community and the youth in parishes with effective youth ministry. For the adult leaders, parish staff members, and youth interviewed for this project, the parish community is very important in their description of effective youth ministry. Without any prompting, these groups repeatedly describe their parish as a home for youth ministry. In different sites around the country, youth and adults use images like "second home," "part of the fabric," and "heart of the parish." They describe in glowing terms their parish's feeling about young people and their parish's support for youth ministry. The leaders in these parish communities have a common vision for youth ministry and work together on behalf of youth.

Five overall findings about the parish community and its relationship to youth ministry emerged from the interviews. These communities care deeply for the youth in their midst, and—as in all healthy relationships—this affection is mutual. Youth also care about the parish and feel connected with adults in the community. One powerful image that leaders used to describe their community is a web of relationships: youth to youth, youth to adults, youth ministry leaders to parents, parents to youth, youth to the parish as a whole. Through this web, youth are served, included, and empowered.

Overall Findings Regarding Parish Support

Let's turn our attention now to the five overall findings that describe how parishes support effective youth ministry. The first paragraph summarizes the finding, and then the finding will be fleshed out with additional comments and quotes from the interviewees.

Parish Support Finding 1: Support from the Whole Parish

Parish youth ministry thrives when it has the support of the whole parish. Parish support is characterized by these general practices and attitudes.

- Youth feel at home in the parish and are genuinely known and liked by parish members.

- Youth are integrated into the full life of the parish. This involvement of youth in parish ministries and parish activities is planned for, encouraged, and affirmed.

- Youth share in leadership and decision-making in parish committees, ministries, and organizations.

- Youth have opportunities to witness to their faith with peers, children, and adults.

- Parish staff and leadership are supportive of youth ministry and youth involvement.

“The parish is where the Church lives. Parishes are communities of faith, of action, and of hope. They are where the Gospel is proclaimed and celebrated, where believers are formed and sent to renew the earth.**”**
(USCCB, Communities of Salt and Light, p. 1)

Parish staff, adult leaders, and youth all concurred that the support of the parish community is crucial to the effectiveness of youth ministry. Youth share that when they experience this support, they feel welcome in the parish. They thrive on meaningful relationships with parish members, both young and old.

> We call it youth ministry but sometimes I think that it should be called community ministry . . . it's not always just the youth, although that's what the main part of it is, but we do stuff for the community so, like,

we're doing community work so it could be just community ministry that we're dealing with.

Youth Participant

Our church is like my second home. It's, like, the best place . . .

Youth Participant

I see a lot of teenagers that really love to be involved in their parishes and youth ministry gives them the opportunity to share their talents with their whole parish and to help build their faith even more. So that when they become adults they'll still want to be involved in their parishes and do even more things because the youth are the future of the church and so starting now we develop an even greater love and want to do the Lord's work.

Youth Participant

Parish staff members describe support for youth as a priority for their community. They identify the support as originating in the affection of adults for the young members of the church. In *Renewing the Vision*, parishes are encouraged to become "youth friendly" (USCCB, *RTV*, p. 13). It is remarkable that the parishes participating in the research are far beyond just being friendly or tolerant of youth: They cherish the youth in their midst. The parish community has become a second home to youth.

Consider this finding that was identified in the interviews with parish staffs: "Parishes with effective youth ministry genuinely like and know youth and show their affection by welcoming them and their contributions, by affirming them, and by encouraging them. Youth feel at home and safe in these parishes." The following quotations from the parish staff interviews show the relationship between this affection for youth and youth's integration in parish life.

The point is, they feel at home, this is their home and they may not come home as often as you'd like them to, every week, or more often, but they know where home is when they need to drop in.

Parish Staff

One more thing that works (in youth ministry) is if you show these kids love. I love them.

Parish Staff

Support is hard to quantify. Adult leaders in these parishes described support in very practical ways. For example, in these communities youth don't just participate in activities or strategies; they are also encouraged to take part in leadership and decision-making for the parish. They are often involved in leadership groups such as parish councils and worship commissions. In these parishes youth have opportunities to witness to their faith with peers, children, and adults. This involvement of youth is encouraged and supported by the parish leadership and the entire parish community.

Here's how some of the adult leaders shared the importance of youth becoming integrated into the parish, which also means that youth have a voice in parish life.

> First and foremost, I think it's comprehensive, meaning that it [youth ministry] is infused; young people are infused in every aspect of the faith community life.
>
> *Adult Leader*

> A lot of people are putting energy into helping kids find ways to be involved in the parish. So when you go to a meeting of the lectors it ranges from 14 to 84, and the same thing with the music ministry.
>
> *Adult Leader*

> So I see them involved in part of the fabric of the parish, of inviting us to come together with each other, but also inviting us to reflect.
>
> *Parish Staff*

"[Parishes] should be a place where [young people] are welcomed, grow in Jesus Christ, and minister side by side with the adults of the community.**"**

(USCCB Committee on the Laity, A Message to Youth, p. 3)

Parish Support Finding 2: A Priority on Youth Ministry

In parishes with effective youth ministry, the parish community understands and places a priority on youth ministry. This is demonstrated by the following characteristics:

- Parishioners know that youth ministry is everyone's responsibility.

- The community desires youth ministry that is infused into parish life.

One thing that marks the communities that participated in this research project is that youth ministry is not separate from parish life. Adult leaders and parish staff members place priority on youth ministry. Many of them described youth ministry as being "at the heart" of their parish: they see ministry to youth as everyone's responsibility. This understanding of youth ministry is matched by a desire on the part of parishioners that youth be included in all elements of parish life. Older parishioners want to get to know the youth and experience the energy and vitality of faith they bring to the community as a whole.

> I think youth ministry in this community is at the heart of what we do as a parish.
>
> *Parish Staff*

> I hope for inclusive community involvement . . . that there is never a thought that says, Oh, what about your youth? It just comes naturally that our youth are invited in, are accepted, and are put to work as vital people in our parish.
>
> *Adult Leader*

Parish Support Finding 3: Balance Between Serving Youth in a Peer Community and Within the Overall Parish

Some goals of youth ministry are best achieved when youth are involved in overall parish life, praying and working together with adults and children. Other goals are best achieved within a youth peer community where youth are relating primarily to other youth. Balancing both these dimensions is important for creating effective youth ministry.

One thing that the parishes involved in the research actively avoid is developing a youth community that is parallel to but separate from the general parish community. Stuart Cummings-Bond describes this approach as "the one-eared Mickey Mouse model of youth ministry" (p. 76). In this model, the congregation as a whole (visualized as a large circle) has an attached but separate youth congregation (visualized by a smaller attached circle). Youth experience belonging, worship, and service as part of a youth congregation running in parallel tracks with the adult congregation. At the end of years of participation in a youth congregation, young people may never make it into the adult congregation because it is foreign to them. The energy, style of worship, and network of relationships are a whole new world that years of youth ministry have not prepared the young person for.

To avoid parallel congregations, some of the most effective parishes in the research project develop a two-pronged approach. They accomplish some goals for youth ministry through involvement of youth in parish life, relying upon the strengths of their particular parish community. They achieve other goals for youth ministry within programs for youth and their peers. One youth ministry coordinator describes this as very liberating; she relies upon the parish's community service program to include youth, which leaves her more time to develop programs and strategies that address other components of youth ministry. One pastor describes this approach as a dance.

> There is a beautiful dance going on between the ministry of youth over on one side, but it is at the same token bringing them in and

If parishes are to be worthy of the loyalty and active participation of youth, they will need to become "youth-friendly" communities in which youth have a conspicuous presence in parish life. These are parish communities that value young people—welcoming them into their midst; listening to them; responding to their needs; supporting them with prayer, time, facilities, and money.

(USCCB, RTV, p. 13)

keeping them part of the larger parish. . . . There is a lot of faith in our youth ministries with that wisdom, I think.

Pastor

Youth ministry is active: I don't care where it is, it has to be across the parish; it has to be active.

Adult Leader

Parish Support Finding 4: Pastor Support

Pastor support for youth ministry is crucial: Some pastors work side by side with other leaders in youth ministry; other pastors are present to youth but work behind the scenes to support and empower the Coordinator of Youth Ministry and the youth ministry team.

Youth, adult leaders, and staff members all acknowledged a common theme: The pastor sets a tone in the parish that enables youth ministry to grow. The importance of this support seems natural, given the integrated nature of youth ministry in these communities. When youth are truly a part of parish life, part of the reason that they feel welcomed and valued is that the pastor is clear in his support.

However, the research indicated that there isn't just one way for pastors to be supportive, which can be a relief to pastors who want to support youth ministry. In some communities, the pastor is one of the youth ministry leaders. Sometimes he was even described as the driving force for dynamic ministry. But in many communities, the pastor acknowledges that he isn't gifted or drawn to work in a special way with youth. These pastors see their main role as supporting the leaders who work with youth.

The pastor lets the youth minister do his or her job. The pastor is good at delegating. The pastor doesn't have to micromanage.

Parish Staff

Support from the other staff and from our pastor is crucial. I mean if you're not getting (support) from the top, you won't get it.

Parish Staff

Adult leaders identified pastor support as crucial and were able to describe the difference they experience when support is present and when it is not. They shared that pastors support youth ministry when they are present at youth activities, learn young people's names, support the program with financial resources, and understand the vision for youth ministry.

> He's there when things are going well and when they're not going well; you can walk through the door and say, "Hey, do you have five minutes, I need some advice for the benefit of the young people," and he loves them as much and they know that.
>
> *Adult Leader*

Parish Support Finding 5: Leaders Work Collaboratively

In parishes with effective youth ministry, the parish staff and leaders support each other and work collaboratively. The boundaries between ministries are permeable, that is, ministries overlap and staff are not rigid or protective about their ministerial areas of responsibility.

In parishes that participated in this project, parish staff and leaders support each other's ministries. This support is nurtured through education and understanding. In one parish, the pastor and staff spoke glowingly about the work the youth ministry coordinator has done to help the staff understand youth ministry. For several months in a row, the youth ministry coordinator presented different parts of the vision for comprehensive youth ministry to the staff in brief presentations. From this work, staff members learned how to include youth and how to think about working with other aspects of youth ministry.

Another mark of these parish leaders is that they work collaboratively, not just in youth ministry. In these communities, youth don't see definite lines or walls between the different ministries; instead, the various ministries of the community work in concert. All of the ministries of the parish are experienced by youth and adults as a common vision. The consistency among ministries and the collaboration of leaders helps youth to feel welcome throughout the various ministries of the parish.

> If you don't have a pastor and a set of directors, or a parish team, that is supporting one another, you have got all kinds of problems. It has to be a team effort all the way.
>
> *Parish Staff*

Having your staff on board makes comprehensive ministry just so much easier because instead of people walking through the door going, "I need you because I need free labor," they come running through the door, going, "Oh, my gosh, I have four high school students signed up to be teachers, and I normally have twenty at this point; where are they?" They rely on them (young people), I mean, they want them badly. Having your staff behind you and you behind them makes a huge difference.

Adult Leader

What we are really trying to emphasize . . . is trying to support each other's ministry. Well, it is not like we come up with the ministry and then you are off all by yourself . . . that is a no-no in our community. Our task is to build community.

Parish Staff

According to the youth and adults interviewed, their parishes understand youth ministry, support youth ministry, and cherish youth in their midst. They also recognize the power and vitality of young people's faith. Youth, adult leaders, and parish staff members all described the impact on the community when youth share their faith and serve the community through liturgical ministries and service roles. Parish staff members describe this powerful witness as follows:

Effective youth ministry unleashes the power of youth faith witness to children, peers, the parish, and the world. Youth's faith witness is vulnerable, bold, eloquent, deep, profound, authentic, vibrant, and moving. It includes, uplifts, and invites.

Parish Staff

Having a young person speak at a liturgy and (experiencing) their spirituality is awe inspiring.

Parish Staff

Recommendations

The parishes that participated in this research describe a vibrant relationship between the parish as a whole and its young members. Whatever the current state of youth ministry in a parish may be, leaders in youth ministry and parish life can take practical steps to develop this relationship. Here are six suggestions:

1: Communicate a vision for youth ministry to the parish staff and the parish community. It is natural that people can best support something that they understand, especially when they can connect an inspiring vision with the values held by members of the community. *Renewing the Vision* is a starting point for describing a vision for youth ministry that is comprehensive, diverse, and integrated within the life of the parish. One youth ministry coordinator shared a vision for youth ministry by working with a team of youth to prepare a presentation about youth ministry that was shared at meetings and gatherings of parish organizations throughout the year. In a different parish, the parish staff considered different aspects of the vision for youth ministry as part of their staff meetings over a series of months.

2: Identify practical ways that the parish community can support youth and youth ministry. In the communities researched by this project, youth felt valued and welcomed in their parish and they felt included in parish life. Everything youth experience in the parish is part of their experience of youth ministry. One of your greatest leadership actions is helping the parish know how to be welcoming, accepting, and supportive of youth. In some parishes, they include bulletin inserts and announcements during liturgy with suggestions for ways that youth can be more welcomed. These attitudes of welcome are nurtured through modeling of parish staff and leadership. You can also keep the

66 *[Parishes] should have programs for [young people] that recognize their special talents and role in the life of the Church. [They] bring to the parish community youthfulness, energy, vitality, hopefulness, and vision.* 99

(USCCB Committee on the Laity, A Message to Youth, p. 3)

community informed about what is happening in the parish's youth ministry efforts and enlist their participation and support.

3: Connect youth to the life of the parish. Youth must be ministered to as part of overall parish life, participating side by side with children and adults. You can gather with other leaders to assess and choose elements of parish life that can become more open to youth participation. This participation doesn't just happen; you need to be intentional about making youth welcome by helping leaders include the needs, interests, and gifts of youth within events and programs.

Many parish events become part of a youth ministry strategy when you are intentional in making sure that youth are included in the prayers, stories, examples, and teaching of the event. For example, the parish mission can be part of the youth ministry's Lenten preparations if you take the time to prepare the mission speaker to speak to youth in the assembly. A simple change can make a big difference; for instance, including chips and sodas along with the donuts and coffee during hospitality time helps youth to know they were thought of.

4: Find ways for youth to be involved in ministry, leadership, and service. Effective youth ministry will include ways to encourage youth to be involved in liturgical and catechetical ministries, leadership for youth ministry, shared leadership in the parish, and community service. These involvements can be introduced by special projects, but for many youth, these involvements may become regular commitments. This is especially important for juniors and seniors in high school who have a lot to contribute and are sometimes more interested in sharing leadership than in being part of an ongoing youth community such as a youth group.

When you involve youth in ministry, leadership, and service, you are connecting them to other adults in the community. Not all adults feel comfortable working with youth and many do not know how to bring out the best in youth service and behavior. That's where ministry leaders who are experienced in working with youth need to take the time to prepare adults who will guide youth in leadership, service, and ministry roles. This kind of practical help can make all of the difference. For instance, in one parish, the youth were invited to become ushers for liturgy, but the adult ushers didn't know how to work effectively with youth. The youth ministry coordinator took the time to meet with the adults and discuss ways to communicate with youth, bring out their best behavior, and guide them in performing this ministry function.

5: Develop collaborative relationships and mutual support for other ministries in the parish. Youth ministry leaders can make a tremendous impact on youth in the parish through openness and collaboration with other leaders. As they envision and plan for youth ministry that is infused within parish life, their leadership role will grow and change. You need to care about the parish as a whole and look for ways to serve youth through all the ministries of the parish community at the same time that you identify ways youth can bring their gifts to the whole parish.

To foster collaboration, take practical steps to support other ministries. Be interested and informed about the ministries in the parish. Share your gifts within other ministries. For instance, if you have a gift for leading prayer or music, offer to help in a program being led by another staff person. Youth ministry leaders also foster collaboration by actively seeking input and consultation from other staff members when planning for youth ministry.

6: Strengthen the relationship between youth ministry and the pastor. The research identified pastor support as crucial, but described different ways for pastors to be supportive of youth ministry. Strengthening the relationship between the pastor and youth ministry helps connect youth to the pastor as the spiritual leader of the community; it also creates a foundation for greater inclusion of youth within the life of the parish. In strengthening this relationship, remember that the pastor is busy and is juggling many different ministry areas. One way to develop this relationship is to invite the pastor to be part of specific aspects within a youth gathering. For instance, you could ask the pastor to come and bless the meal that is part of the retreat day.

Another strategy is to develop a regular pattern of communicating with the pastor about youth ministry. Ask for a short meeting monthly or every other week. Come to this meeting prepared with a written list of items that you want to share. If decisions or recommendations from the pastor were discussed, send him a note or e-mail following your conversation that summarizes the key points and decisions. Include leadership youth and members of the leadership team in prayer support and writing encouraging notes to the pastor throughout the year.

A note to pastors: The key to supporting youth ministry is prayerful support and presence. Support doesn't mean you have to be the youth minister or that you need to emulate other pastors for whom involvement in youth ministry is a large part of their ministry. In your own style, find a way to get to know young people, be present to the youth ministry community, be supportive of the youth ministry leaders, and lead the way to include youth within the life of the parish.

Conclusion

Youth, youth ministry, and the parish community all thrive when youth are connected to the parish. Youth thrive because they experience consistency between their experiences of youth ministry events and parish participation, and they benefit from the relationships of an intergenerational community. Youth ministry thrives because leaders can rely upon aspects of parish life and other adults in the community to accomplish some of the goals for youth ministry. The parish community benefits because parish life is enriched by the energy, enthusiasm, and gifts of young members.

In this project, the adults, youth, and parish staff members described parishes that care about youth, include youth, and work together on young people's behalf. Hearing about this integrated practice of youth ministry can be empowering if the parish seems ready for this kind of relationship. On the other hand, this insight can be frustrating to leaders in communities that are not supportive and not collaborative. The first step is to assess the situation of the community. Once the parish identifies its strengths and weaknesses, a plan can be created to develop support. To be effective, youth ministry leaders need to be intentional about the work of building support and inspiring a community to work together on behalf of youth.

A parish is the place where you live your lives in community as disciples. Despite the weaknesses or challenges in your community, making the effort to forge a strong relationship between youth and the parish is worth your best efforts, prayers, and leadership.

Assessment Questions

When working with the parish staff, leadership groups, and the leadership team for youth ministry, consider the following questions in assessing your community.

Parish Support for Youth Ministry

- How well does our parish know and value our youth?

- How are youth involved in overall parish life?

- In what ministries and aspects of parish life could youth become involved?

- In what ways are youth involved in leadership and decision-making in the parish?

- In what ways do we encourage and affirm youth involvement in parish life?

- How well does our parish understand youth ministry?

Parish Staff

- How well does our parish staff understand youth ministry and know about our youth ministry efforts?

- How well does our parish staff collaborate?

- In what ways do we make an effort to communicate with and involve our pastor in youth ministry efforts?

The Qualities of Effective Youth Ministry

The research findings revealed some specific qualities that are part of effective youth ministry. The findings indicated that effective youth ministry responds to young people's lives and needs. It is marked by variety, hospitality, and innovation. Youth have ownership and help lead the ministry, and families feel connected and included. These qualities of effective practices in youth ministry confirmed many foundational principles that have guided youth ministry in the United States over the past two decades. But where these foundational principles often sounded like abstract theory, in parishes with effective youth ministry they are embodied in identifiable concrete practices.

As you will see in looking at the following research findings, in these parishes the entire parish community desires a youth ministry that is infused into the mainstream life of the parish. They have imagined and put into practice a graceful dance that incorporates a distinctive ministry to youth and the involvement of young people in ministry throughout the whole of parish life.

Overall Findings Regarding Qualities

Five overall findings describe the qualities of effective youth ministry. These findings highlight the way youth are ministered to within parish life and the way that youth experience ministry with their peers. The first paragraph summarizes the finding, and then the finding will be fleshed out with additional comments and quotes from the interviewees.

Qualities Finding 1: Ministry is Responsive and Innovative

Effective youth ministry responds to the real lives, needs, and interests of youth.

- Youth feel like they matter.

- Ministry is innovative and dynamic.

- There is not one model—in these parishes there is a relational pattern of knowing youth, innovating, and changing in order to be responsive.

"I [Paul] planted, Apollos watered, but God gave the growth.**"**

(1 Corinthians 3:6)

In parishes with effective youth ministry, youth experience ministry as beginning with caring relationships. As with Jesus' approach to those he encountered, effective youth ministry starts with the real needs of the person who encounters Christ. If they are hungry, they are fed. If they are hurting, they are healed. An open, accepting environment is the starting point. The Good News of your faith is then connected to the real-life issues and everyday interests of youth. By starting with their life, ministry engages young people's energy and helps them make connections to the faith story and to each other.

If it is something they are interested in, then we cover the material. It really sparked something this year, and people are actually wanting to come to youth night . . . you really have to know your audience, and if you know what you are talking about, they will get excited about it, and they will come.
Youth Participant

A welcoming environment and loving and supporting environment in which a young person within the group is able to feel like they have a place, and they have a voice, and that they count in who they are, and what they are, and what they dream, and what they think matters.

Parish Staff

When youth ministry responds to their real lives, needs, and interests, youth feel like they matter. This dynamic needs to be innovative and creative; there is not one model, but rather a pattern of changing in order to be responsive to youth. The leadership creates ministry by experimenting, taking risks, and trying again. This type of responsiveness allows current events in the world and in the community to become part of the ministry. This aspect was a finding from the adult leaders: Parishes with effective youth ministry provide timely opportunities for young people to pray and talk when crisis strikes—particularly when the crisis is the death of someone they know. Youth, adults, and parish staff members all described variety and responsiveness as very important.

Asking for feedback on the things you do. Why is that important? Because if you are doing something that people don't like, you should be able to change.

Youth Participant

They [the youth] wanted variety in their program. They did not want to just do worksheets and books, nor just sit in the classroom the whole time. It was interesting to find out what their interests were, what they wanted to see come out of the program.

Adult Leader

So we joke about it but it is like experiment number 793. We shift if things don't go the way we thought they would go. You have to be flexible. Shifting position and the direction is very important because there is very little ultimately that doesn't work out.

Parish Staff Member

Qualities Finding 2: Hospitality and Relationship Building

Hospitality and relationship building are foundational to effective youth ministry.

- Young people are welcomed and accepted.

- Leaders extend personal invitations, provide a warm welcome, build relationships, and form groups. These efforts are intentional and ongoing.

- Youth are ministered to within a web of relationships: youth with youth, youth with adults, parish community with youth, and youth in their families.

"Community life is nurtured when the atmosphere is welcoming, comfortable, safe, and predictable—one in which all adolescents know that their presence is welcomed, their energy is appreciated, and their contributions are valued."

(USCCB, RTV, p. 35)

Hospitality extends the circle of belonging. Having inclusive groups is part of an effective youth ministry, groups that welcome any and all youth regardless of race, social status, personalities, physical abilities, or religious background. When youth ministry is open to all cultures and categories of young people, youth develop an openness and appreciation for diversity. This openness attracts youth and breaks down barriers. In the interviews, youth share their concern that cliques in youth ministry activities are a problem and an obstacle. A resolve for inclusiveness and a practice of "all youth have a home here" produces awesome, fun, amazing youth ministry that is a blessing to the whole parish.

I hope that one day there will be no color barriers. It gives me hope to know that one day somebody will just wake up and see that God or whoever they believe in is the answer to the majority, actually to all their problems, and we can create and have faith in God.

Youth Participant

Adult leaders and youth observed that teenagers enjoy building relationships with Catholic teenagers from other parishes. Effective parish youth ministry enables this through inter-parish retreats, social events, and diocesan activities. This requires a non-competitive, non-possessive attitude on the part of the youth ministers.

> That is all they talk about, is seeing their friends from the other parishes. They go to several of these groups now. They don't just go to mine.
>
> *Adult Leader*

> I found a huge dynamic lately where our kids want to be with kids from other parishes and go on to the universal look of the Catholic Church.
>
> *Adult Leader*

Being intentional and deliberate about building life-giving relationships means building and nurturing small groups. An open, accepting youth community helps young people connect with their peers as people of faith and supports their quest to learn more about their faith.

> Our staff and leaders are being conscious . . . about the culture of being intentional and deliberate about building relationships, and that is the thing that we really emphasize.
>
> *Parish Staff*

> Monday nights excite me because I know I have a lot of homework, but I get to go to the peer ministry group and I am going to see all my friends.
>
> *Youth Participant*

Youth ministry develops loving, caring relationships among youth and adults. These friendships bring youth closer to God and help youth experience a sense of family within the community.

> It is important to know people in our faith . . . because you develop that closeness where you know this is my friend and she's like me. And you know, this is something we can share together.
>
> *Youth Participant*

Effective youth ministers have a passion for reaching youth who are marginalized or at-risk. They befriend those youth who are rejected by their peers, and they reach out to youth who cause trouble.

Those are the kids that I find the most interesting. Often times they think on their own, they have a little bit of an edge. They introduced me to other kids on the fringe. Everybody is looking for a place that they can belong.

Adult Leader

Qualities Finding 3: Variety of Ways to Be Involved

Effective youth ministry has a variety of ways for youth to be involved. The boundaries between ministries are permeable so that youth can easily be connected to different parish ministries. The parish provides opportunities for different levels of participation in parish life for youth and their families.

"Adolescents today are growing up in a culturally diverse society. The perceived image of the United States has shifted from a melting pot to a multihued tapestry. The strength and beauty of the tapestry lie in the diverse colors and textures of its component threads—the values and traditions claimed by the different racial and ethnic groups that constitute the people of the United States."

(USCCB, RTV, p. 22)

Youth ministry provides numerous, varied activities that enable young people to be engaged in the youth ministry programs and parish life. It balances the social, educational, formational, sacramental, and service dimensions. It is permeable, which means there are no boundaries or protected turf that prevent youth from participating in different aspects of youth ministry and parish life. Effective parishes provide many opportunities for young people to get involved in youth ministry and parish life on a variety of different levels, with a variety of activities and experiences, encouraging greater participation.

This variety also allows youth with different schedules, needs, and interests to belong at their own pace. Like adults, youth grow in their discipleship in their own time and style. Variety in youth ministry includes activities, groups, and involvements that can attend to youth who are at different levels of spiritual maturity and faith development.

> Effectiveness in our youth ministry is credited to the multifaceted nature of the program. Not only does it make it a holistic program, but also it enables the program to tap into different young people who will respond to different things.
>
> *Parish Staff*

> I really like how we have a lot of different levels of participation.
>
> *Youth Participant*

Qualities Finding 4: Youth Ownership and Leadership

In parishes with effective youth ministry, youth are active in and have ownership in the parish's youth ministry. They are not just passive recipients of ministry by adults. Youth share leadership for visioning and implementing programs and strategies. They witness to their faith with their peers. By leading programs, youth grow in their own faith.

Youth are willing, excited, passionate leaders in parishes that provide them with opportunities to explore various leadership roles and empower them to be in ministry with their peers and the whole parish. Young people share their gifts and energy as leaders in parish life. Leading programs helps youth grow in their faith and appreciate the growth of their peers' faith.

In parishes with effective youth ministry, young people have ownership of the ministry. The benefits of this ownership include growth in their own faith and increased self-esteem. They become active in the parish and develop as religious leaders who make choices for vocations or careers in church ministry. Leadership training helps young people grow in self-confidence and provides them with helpful skills and knowledge to interact and communicate more effectively. When older teens lead programs or events for younger teens, it gives them the opportunity to impact younger teens' lives and experience personal growth themselves. Young people are doing surprising things in parishes when given the opportunity to lead. All the adult ministers need to do is encourage the youth to take ownership, provide leadership training and formation, and then get out of the way.

> I see it as a way that they're being developed as religious leaders, especially through the leadership part of the youth ministry program.
>
> *Parish Staff*

> That's something that I really find in my work with the youth. I really try to let them think about a vocation in the church.
>
> *Adult Leader*

> What gives me hope is seeing young people graduating from college and choosing careers because of their faith.
>
> *Adult Leader*

Youth share leadership not only in the tasks of ministry but also as witnesses to their faith. Effective ministry unleashes the power of youth faith witness to help young people grow in their own faith and to touch the hearts of peers and the entire faith community. Parish staff members describe youth's faith witness as vulnerable, bold, eloquent, deep, profound, authentic, vibrant, and moving. Opportunities for youth to witness to their faith help them to continue to grow and help other youth connect to the faith story.

> Recently, someone told me that if there were more Christians like me in the world then they would actually consider being Christian. That was probably the best compliment that I have ever got in my entire

"Ministry with adolescents creates flexible and adaptable program structures that address the changing needs and life situations of today's young people and their families within a particular community. **"**

(USCCB, RTV, p. 25)

life. It made me feel really great and just because of youth ministry, I understand my faith more.

Youth Participant

Qualities Finding 5: Connecting with Families

Partnership with families is critical in effective youth ministry. Effective leaders connect with families by providing the following support services:

- Consistent communication about youth ministry

- Relationship building with parents

- Opportunities for parent and family involvement

- Family-based activities and resources

In the views of the adult leaders and parish staff members, parents of teens should be connected to the parish's youth ministry. This connection is nurtured by the attitude of the youth ministry leaders and by practical actions such as consistent communication with parents. Parents can support their children's involvement if they understand how their son or daughter will be involved and if they know what the ministry is trying to accomplish.

If you work with just the youth, it just doesn't work. You have to work with the whole family.

Parish Staff

You trust what is happening. As a parent, that is why you feel better. It isn't just that I trust our youth minister—he isn't going to let anything go wrong. It is more than that. . . . There is a dynamic among the young people that is extreme; it transforms people.

Parish Staff

Family and parent involvement was important in the interviews from a variety of perspectives. Adult leaders noted that they want to be allies with parents in the faith formation of teens, but these efforts are challenging when parents do not know their role in the faith formation process. Parish staff members note that parents often feel inadequate in forming the faith of their children. They see a great need in their communities for adult education in the faith. Youth shared that when their parents are involved at the parish and are open in sharing their faith, this enthusiasm is contagious. Sometimes, for parents who are not active in their faith, youth ministry involvement for their child is a turning point in their own participation and faith growth.

> I see youth ministry as a Christ-centered means of the parish partnering with the families, especially with the parents in helping them to foster and pass on the Catholic faith to their children.
>
> *Adult Leader*

> A real surprise for us is the number of parents that are like, "Tell me what to do with my kid; don't tell me about religion, tell me what to do with my kid the rest of the time." It's been very successful for us. It has met people where they're at.
>
> *Adult Leader*

> The parents go to the same thing we do. And it's like they know . . . what we're talking about. So you can go home and . . . talk to your mom and dad.
>
> *Youth Participant*

> That was really strange, but I think she experienced a similar thing that youth ministry changed her life. She realized that she has been a housewife and a mom for so long she didn't feel like she was doing anything. Youth ministry, it brought my mom back to life. It gave her back to me.
>
> *Youth Participant*

66*Effective ministry with adolescents provides developmentally appropriate experiences, programs, activities, strategies, resources, content, and processes to address the unique developmental and social needs of young and older adolescents.*99

(USCCB, RTV, p. 20)

Recommendations

These qualities of effective youth ministry also address a variety of issues: responsiveness to young people's needs, hospitality, variety, youth leadership, and family participation. To be part of a parish's youth ministry requires the participation of a variety of people: youth, parents, youth ministry leaders, parish staff, and the entire parish community. Consider these suggestions to improve the quality of youth ministry in your community.

1: Identify the realities in the lives of young people today and respond to the real needs and interests of youth with innovative programming. When youth ministry is responding to the real-life situations of young people today, then it will be effective in transforming lives. To get started in becoming more responsive to youth, listen to young people and their parents. Take the time to ask youth what their concerns, questions, needs, and interests are. Stay current in understanding adolescents by making an effort to read and learn about the characteristics and needs of youth today. You can compare this big picture with your personal experiences and conversations with youth and their families.

To be responsive to the needs you identify, create niche activities that may attract small numbers of youth according to their interests. Innovation like this involves risk—as leaders, be gentle with yourselves when events don't attract youth at first. Relationships are the key to this style of programming, so know your youth and provide the gospel message in ways that they understand.

2: Develop the variety and flexibility of the youth ministry involvements in your parish. Most parishes will have a primary ministry effort, such as a youth group or religious education program for youth. This primary effort needs to be complemented by other ways that youth can be part of the parish and its youth ministry. Begin by evaluating your current efforts. How can youth be involved in your community? What opportunities are present for youth who are hesitant to be involved? What is there for youth who want to be challenged and grow? Much of the variety that parishes can provide is created by making room for youth to participate side-by-side with adults in parish activities and ministries. Other variety is created through the development of niche programs that respond to the needs and interests of youth.

3: Provide a variety of opportunities for youth to share leadership and become integral parts of the life and mission of the parish. Youth ministry is a time of apprenticeship when young people can come to know how their particular gifts and talents can be used to benefit the whole faith community. You can do this by providing young leaders with basic training for such things as leading small groups, steps in planning activities, and other leadership skills. Be sure that teams of youth and adults plan and implement major events such as retreats and mission trips. Encourage other organizations and councils to include youth by inviting young people to serve on their committees or by consulting youth when important issues arise. Send key youth leaders to diocesan-sponsored youth leadership training events.

4: Work with parish staff and leadership to eliminate barriers for youth involvement. Parishes stated that ministry boundaries should be permeable and flexible. This requires trust, collaboration, and intentional leadership. Gather with parish staff and ministry leaders to discuss ways that youth can become more involved. Identify practical ways to encourage youth involvement across the ministries throughout parish life.

5: Create an environment of welcome and inclusiveness. A hallmark of Catholic youth ministry should be hospitality. All are welcomed; all are given the same respect and dignity appropriate to their status as a son or daughter of God. Talk to youth in your parish. Find out when they feel welcomed and when they don't. Develop a hospitality team that takes responsibility for helping all youth to feel welcomed and included. Take time each time you meet as leaders to evaluate and plan for hospitality as an integral dimension of everything in youth ministry.

6: Communicate with parents about youth ministry, and provide strategic resources and programs for families. To become partners with parents, you need to take the time to help them know what is happening and what is available. Consider providing a monthly or quarterly youth ministry newsletter for parents. Include information about youth ministry consistently in the parish bulletin—youth do not always read the bulletin, but parents usually do. Gather a group of parents to discuss ways that youth ministry can provide more support. These efforts don't mean that you turn all of youth ministry into family ministry—but it does mean that you help parents know you are there to support them and you want to work with them in ministry with youth.

Conclusion

Effective youth ministry is marked by a number of qualities that must be planned for and made an integrated part of a parish's community life. Ministry marked by these qualities is transformative for both the youth who participate and for the larger parish faith community. Young people in these parishes are challenged to take risks and develop their own confidence. They are given opportunities to explore various leadership roles. The parish creates an atmosphere where all are welcomed, diversity is appreciated, the marginalized are sought out, and the family is seen as a partner in ministry. It is in these communities that young people are seen as both the weavers of ministry as well as those who are woven into the fabric of a parish's overall ministry.

Assessment Questions

Parish staff and youth ministry teams should consider the following questions as a way to assess the qualities of youth ministry in their ministry to youth.

- How responsive is our youth ministry to the real lives, needs, and interests of youth?

- How is our ministry innovative in responding to youth's needs?

- How are we nurturing the web of relationships in our community (youth with youth, youth with adults, parish community with youth, youth in their families)?

- How does our parish and its youth ministry respond to the diversity of youth in our community?

- Are there a variety of ways for youth to be involved in our parish and its youth ministry efforts?

- How are we involving youth in leading youth ministry and promoting ownership of the ministry among the youth?

- How are we communicating and connecting with parents of adolescents?

- How are we providing strategic programs and resources that support families of youth?

## CHAPTER 3

The Program Elements of Effective Youth Ministry

One of the surprises that came out of the research project was how much emphasis was placed on things that were not activities, events, or meetings. Some of the researchers expected that most of the discussion in the interviews would center on specific youth activities or parish programs. As you can see by the chapters in this book, the emphasis in the interview discussions more often focused on parish attitudes, qualities, and the leadership that undergirds effective youth ministry.

This doesn't mean that participants did not discuss specific activities and program elements. Youth, adult leaders, and parish staffs all identified events they had experienced as being particularly effective. In fact, it was interesting to see the convergence of all three groups on some particular program elements: faith formation, service, liturgy, retreats, and extended trips. A great deal of enthusiasm and energy was evident when the discussion turned to these. Looking more closely at the findings will reveal their benefits and characteristics.

Note: There can be a lot of confusion in people's understanding of the terms "programs," "program elements," and "ministry components." In this chapter, "youth ministry program" refers to all the activities and strategies a parish uses to minister to its youth. By this definition, a parish cannot have more than one youth ministry program. "Program elements" are specific types of activity that are integral and ongoing parts of a parish's youth ministry program. Published catechetical and youth ministry resources may be program elements, but they are not the parish's youth ministry program. "Ministry components" are the eight fundamental ways of ministering effectively with adolescents as defined in *Renewing the Vision*: advocacy, catechesis, community life, evangelization, justice and service, leadership development, pastoral care, and prayer and worship. A program element may encompass one or more ministry components.

Overall Findings on Effective Program Elements

Let's turn our attention now to the five program elements that the research participants identified as particularly important. For each element, the first paragraph summarizes the finding, then the finding will be fleshed out with additional comments and quotes from the interviewees.

Program Finding 1: Faith Formation

> **"**Generally youth catechesis should be proposed in new ways which are open to the sensibilities and problems of this age group.**"**
>
> (USCCB, General Directory for Catechesis, p. 176)

Faith formation is a key component in many parishes with effective youth ministry. But young people often perceive faith formation as boring and out-of-touch with their lived reality. Effective faith formation with adolescents has to be engaging and connect faith to youth's life experience. Participants identified the following elements in effective faith formation:

- Is facilitated by open-minded, authentic, faith-filled adults

- Includes community building

- Includes peer sharing, peer witness, and youth leadership

- Teaches about Catholic identity

- Seizes teachable moments

- Is experiential, active, and innovative

- Doesn't feel like school

Parish staff members and adult leaders presumed that faith formation or religious education was an essential part of youth ministry. As one parish staff member stated, "The quality of our religious education is really top notch. I think that is the key to having a successful youth ministry as opposed to just youth community building." Yet the young people in the interviews were clear that faith formation classes were at times a negative part of the parish's youth ministry.

> It's so awful. If people go through eight, nine years of that you just finally get to the point where you're like, all right, enough. We made our Confirmation in the 8th grade. . . . I'm done with that.
>
> *Youth Participant*

> They don't even come because they're burnt out with CCD. I think maybe if CCD wasn't so . . . awful and boring.
>
> *Youth Participant*

The adult youth ministry leaders were certainly aware of this reaction. While not claiming to have all the answers, they seemed sure of three things. First, catechesis has to be integrated into all the activities and components of youth ministry, not just weekly classes. Second, catechesis has to connect the content and doctrine of faith to the life experiences of young people. Third, to be effective, catechesis has to be innovative.

> That group of boys I talked about earlier? There's no way . . . I can set those boys down and do a religious education class with them. But do you know how much catechesis we've done by playing basketball together?
>
> *Adult Leader*

> The key is that we allow them to experience the message. It's not boring. You know, they come in and experience the message. We don't just open a book and read it to them . . . they live the message, somehow or other, through what we do.
>
> *Adult Leader*

> Our religious education director said: "What do you mean, tear the roof off this thing? It was invented 1,500 years ago. You just have to follow the plan." But we find that youth ministry works when we don't stick with a single plan. We constantly try to find better ways to bring these kids to Jesus.
>
> *Adult Leader*

The young people also repeatedly emphasized the importance of helping them connect faith to life.

> In my church, youth ministry is like a bridge to connect the lakes of the real world, Church, and God.
>
> *Youth Participant*

> That's the point . . . that we can take this faith, or idea, or these lessons that we're supposed to learn, or these things we're supposed to believe and say, "How do these things go into our lives?"
>
> *Youth Participant*

Program Finding 2: Extended Trips

Activities that involve taking extended time away from the parish create special moments for ministry to and with young people. These include events such as work camps, leadership camps, diocesan and national conferences, and World Youth Day. Not only participation in the event itself, but also the travel time led to these benefits:

- Being part of a large, Catholic event helped the young people feel pride and enthusiasm in being Catholic.

- A deep sense of community is built between youth who didn't previously know each other and between youth and their adult leaders.

- The event creates opportunities for youth and adults to take on leadership roles and grow in their leadership abilities.

66 *World Youth Day is the Church's Day for youth and with youth. This idea is not an alternative to ordinary youth ministry, often carried out with great sacrifice and self-denial. Indeed it intends actually to consolidate this work by offering new encouragement for commitment, objectives which foster ever greater involvement and participation.* 99

(Pope John Paul II, Letter of Pope John Paul II to Cardinal Eduardo Francisco Pironio)

- Young people are awestruck by the larger sense of Church and the large number of Catholic youth they are connected with across the nation and across the globe.

The young people in the interviews were the most vocal about the impact that such trips had on their pride in being Catholic. They often described experiences such as national conferences and World Youth Day with words such as "incredible," "shocking," and "amazing." Comments such as the following were typical.

It's just amazing to see that there's all these people who have the same beliefs and the same ideas as you. You might think, Well, gee, I'm the only one or whatever. When you go there are thousands of people who all think very similar to you. You realize that you're not alone.

Youth Participant

There are workshops where 33,000 people are Catholic and they are proud of it. . . . It's an incredible experience to see that many people proud to say that they love Jesus.

Youth Participant

Although adult leaders acknowledged the importance of providing their youth with these experiences of the universal Church, their focus was more personal. They experienced trips as unique opportunities to build deeper relationships with youth.

It's the . . . getting dirty and crabby and cranky, and getting happy and glad—all of it. It's really cool.

Adult Leader

So stick me on a bus, send me across the country and I'm a happy camper. . . . When you face the challenges of travel with someone, you really get to know that person. You share with them on a completely different level than you would share with them in normal situations.

Adult Leader

Program Finding 3: Liturgy

Young people hunger for experiences of liturgy that engage the whole person. They look for movement and spontaneity, musical styles they identify with, ritual that engages all the senses, and homilies that speak to their life experience. Parishes with effective youth ministry respond by incorporating these needs into the parish's celebration of liturgy.

These parishes also actively include youth in liturgical ministries. This is seen as a tremendous value to the parish community. Youth bring energy, needed skills, and their powerful presence to the parish's liturgical life. Liturgical involvement helps young people grow in confidence, in faith, and in developing their gifts.

"Even a single program or strategy can incorporate several of the ministry components, as in the case of a retreat program."

(USCCB, RTV, p. 26)

A surprising finding in the interviews with young people is the emphasis they placed on liturgy that was sensual. They were quite articulate in naming the liturgical experience they desired. The young people also felt that being involved in liturgical ministries helped them uncover their gifts, connected them to the parish community, and gave them a deeper understanding of liturgy.

Mass is supposed to be a sensual experience, not sensual in any sense you might be thinking, but touching the five senses. We should be praising God with our entire bodies. With our hands, we need to clap, we need to sing. Mass should be joyful.
Youth Participant

If God were to walk right into this room . . . we would want to worship him with all our body, with all our senses, our mind, our being, and that's what I think we're trying to get at the teen Mass.

Youth Participant

The way I strengthen and show my faith is at Church I play bongos and drums. . . . It's this crazy vibe I get when everybody just has big smiles on their faces at the end of the song. Everyone is enjoying Mass.

Youth Participant

Adult leaders and parish staff focused on the importance of liturgy that was responsive to young people's spiritual needs. They were critical of liturgy that did not take those needs into account. These leaders were enthusiastic in describing the value of youth involvement in liturgical ministries for the whole community.

Another thing that is not working is the boring homily. I think it's an insult to young people if he (the priest) cannot include the whole parish when speaking on a subject. He should speak to the youth as well as the adults.

Adult Leader

If young people look up to the altar and don't see anyone their own age, that says to them, "I am not a part of this."

Adult Leader

I am also impressed, when it comes to liturgy on Sunday morning, this is one parish where we have a tremendous number of high school students involved. . . . The pride they take in that, the friendliness they bring to it, and the respect they have . . . the parish is really proud of them.

Parish Staff

Program Finding 4: Retreats

Youth retreats have a unique ability to touch the hearts of young people. Retreat experiences help build communities of faith, help youth grow closer to God, and draw them back into active involvement in parish life. Simply put, retreats have the power to change the lives of young people, calling them more deeply into discipleship.

I think every single time I go on a retreat I get closer to God. . . . In between the retreats sometimes I drift away [from God]. But whenever I go on retreat I get time to sit and think and pray and read the Bible.

Youth Participant

The fact that retreats can be a powerful experience for young people is hardly news for anyone who has been active in youth ministry. But it was an extraordinary experience to hear young people speak about the life-changing impact that retreats have on their spiritual lives. In fact, the youth most often talked about their relationship with God when describing a retreat experience.

Immersion experiences, service projects and justice education programs present opportunities for youth to see the face of Jesus in the marginalized, oppressed and poor.

(The Challenge of Catholic Youth Evangelization, p. 20)

Basically I was probably a sophomore when I accidentally ended up on this retreat that I thought was the Confirmation retreat and it wasn't. My mom drove me up and we had already paid so I was like, OK, I guess I will go. That was the experience of a lifetime. Suddenly my faith was so much more real for me. I really became like a part of the family.

Youth Participant

It was a definite growing-closer-to-God time in my life. I have always prayed before meals, when you go to bed, things like that, but then I just started talking to God in prayer. It was such a great weekend for me and such a big eye-opener to how much God is in my life and how He is in everything in the world.

Youth Participant

Besides providing significant faith experiences, adult leaders also identified retreats as opportunities for building community and involving young people in leadership.

> We have multiple ministries, but our main ministry—and it's the ministry everybody wants to be on—is the retreat ministry. Because it's the sharing of faith ministry. And they [peer leaders] grow by their sharing.
>
> *Adult Leader*

> The retreats are huge and successful, empowering and connecting. They grab even the most difficult kids.
>
> *Parish Staff*

Program Finding 5: Service

Participating in Christian service has a powerful impact in the faith life of Catholic teens. Christian service experiences make Catholic faith real and alive for young people. These experiences foster growth in faith and often change the lives of young people, sometimes dramatically. Some of the changes reported are as follows:

- Changes young people's perspective on the poor

- Broadens their awareness of the causes of social injustice

- Creates empathy for others

- Helps young people feel valuable, that they can make a difference

> They [volunteers in a homeless shelter] cared so much for other people, more than I ever did. They saw each other as equals. They would willingly go out and help these other people even though they had, by our standards, so little to give. So here I am thinking, "Ho, I am such a good great person spending three or four hours trying to help these people." I realized that in my own way, maybe I didn't need the same kind of monetary help, but I needed just as much support and spiritual help as they did.
>
> *Youth Participant*

I definitely saw Christ in the people we served. It didn't matter what they were doing. I understood why Jesus includes outcasts in his ministry because these kids are the kids that people in society don't really want.

Youth Participant

This finding for Christian service is similar to the finding on retreats because the interviews reflected a similar, life-changing aspect connected to this program element. The difference, of course, is that while the retreats are often inward-focused, the experience of service is outward-focused. Adult leaders and parish staff members recognize that service provides opportunities to evangelize youth and intentionally sought to provide opportunities for young people to build relationships with people different from themselves.

Helping young people put themselves in other people's places, as we did in our trip to Mexico last summer; this really has a whole life-long learning effect on those kids. I see that kind of thing having a real long-term effect.

Parish Staff

We put them in a position where they are going to be able to make relationships with the people they are working with . . . suddenly language doesn't matter. They are able to communicate and they get information from people and they build a relationship.

Adult Leader

A strong formational element was part of the Christian service opportunities offered by

"Greater youth participation in the liturgy will not happen without an intentional effort to seek and encourage it. Parents, pastors, parish priests, youth and youth leaders, liturgy committees, and concerned individuals need to create a local pastoral plan."

(National Federation for Catholic Youth Ministry, From Age to Age, p. 2)

## CHAPTER 4

Leadership for Effective Youth Ministry

The research strongly indicated that having the right leadership is an essential ingredient of effective youth ministry. Parish staff members reported that their coordinators of youth ministry fostered youth and adult leadership. Adult leaders talked about the importance of parish support and the impact that their parish staffs have on youth ministry. The young people named the personal attributes they value in their leaders, both youth and adult. Coordinators of youth ministry, adult volunteers, youth, pastors, and parish staff all play an important leadership role within youth ministry. In parishes with effective youth ministry, all of these groups work together to create a vibrant place for youth within the parish.

From the five findings in this chapter, two themes emerge. The first is a description of the attitudes, actions, and qualities of the coordinator of youth ministry. Symposium participants describe a new understanding for this important leadership role, preferring to name these leaders as animators of youth ministry. The coordinator of youth ministry role description implies that the role is primarily programmatic. But those interviewed emphasized the spiritual significance of this leader and the evolving role as the person who inspires and supports ministries throughout parish life. Because of this emphasis, the title of *animator* was suggested. Animator is frequently used to describe ministry leadership in religious communities. The animator knows that he or she is responsible for vision and inspiration as well as coordinating the tasks. The animator is not necessarily in the spotlight when ministry happens, allowing other leaders to emerge and shine.

A second theme in this chapter is the description of the qualities and actions of all adults who work with youth. Youth who encounter adults of vibrant faith grow in their faith and in their sense of belonging within the community. The openness and faithfulness of the adults they encounter in the parish is a key factor for youth. It determines whether youth will choose to participate and how much they will grow in faith and discipleship. Good formation and support of adult leaders enables them to be successful in their roles.

Overall Findings Regarding Leadership for Youth Ministry

Coordinators of Youth Ministry

Three findings are directly related to the role of the coordinator of youth ministry. It should be noted that the "coordinator" is not necessarily a full-time, paid minister.

Leadership Finding 1: Coordinators Hold a Vision for the Ministry

The leadership of effective coordinators of youth ministry is based in an understanding of Church mission, values, reflection on the ministry components of youth ministry, and an understanding of comprehensive youth ministry. They know that youth ministry is the responsibility of the whole parish. Coordinators represent a variety of ages and personalities. What unites them is that they all act from a sense of vocation and awareness that they are called to this ministry.

Effective coordinators regularly check their ministry efforts against a shared parish vision for youth ministry, their own personal goals for their ministry, and *Renewing the Vision*. In addition, effective coordinators are able to set clear direc-

"The future of humanity is in the hands of those who are capable of providing coming generations with reasons for living and hoping."

(Pope Paul VI, Pastoral Constitution on the Church in the Modern World)

The young people who participated in the interviews were very direct in naming the importance of the personality of the youth minister. In their minds, "A youth-friendly youth minister is essential for effective youth ministry." Youth know that without a good coordinator, youth ministry at their parish will falter. As one young leader stated,

> One of the things that really helps is that she is not hypocritical. She lives the life, which is really good. Because I've seen other youth ministers say one thing and then do another thing, or say "We're going to get the kids involved" and then lead everything. So that's one great thing—to follow through with what you say and a lot of personal communication.

Parish staff members are also quite vocal about the importance of coordinators being healthy, well-balanced people, recognizing that the dedication and virtues of the coordinator had a profound impact on the effectiveness of the youth ministry. Hiring the right person was important to the parish staff. As one parish staff member explained:

> When parishes look for youth ministers they have to look for healthy, well-balanced people who don't have particular leanings towards any one ideology and they then are able to bring the health and balance to the whole program. I think attracting the right talent and person is crucial.
> *Parish Staff*

Leadership Finding 3: Coordinators Animate Youth Ministry

Coordinators of youth ministry animate dynamic ministry with youth in a variety of ways. They are especially valued because they invite and welcome youth and adults and make them feel comfortable. Coordinators advocate for young people's place in the church, the programming that youth need. They network with other youth ministers and connect to other parishes and the diocese.

Effective coordinators have the ability to make people feel "at home" within the church and at youth ministry events. They know the importance of remembering names, initiating conversation, and encouraging participation.

We sent out personal invitations and letters, just explaining what we were going to try to do this year and that we would really like to see them come back. We know they couldn't come to everything and to try something and our numbers have tripled, so I just think that personal invitation extended to them really helped our program.

Adult Leader

I think something about our youth minister that really helps is that he is almost like a friend to us. He'll talk to you and he makes you feel comfortable and he's nice to everyone and he'll act like he has known them forever. He always remembers your name. He is sort of like a friend and you really feel like you can laugh and talk with him. He makes you feel comfortable.

Youth Participant

This ability to build relationships extends to parents and other parish adults and includes parish organizations.

We value his ability to invite . . . the parents, who may not . . . feel comfortable in that situation. He invites them in and he learns what they may not know about themselves, or where they might fit in some part of the ministry.

Parish Staff

Adult youth ministry leaders talk about "playing the numbers game." They are frustrated when the number of young people who attend an event becomes the measure for successful youth ministry. They know that it is important to minister to whoever walks through the door on a particular day.

"Ministry coordinators alert the whole community to its responsibility for young people, draw forth the community's gifts and resources, and encourage and empower the community to minister with young people.**"**

(USCCB, RTV, p. 25)

So often, especially at the beginning of youth ministry, we focus so much on numbers because people tell us we need to focus on that. Instead of focusing on the numbers, focus on who is there . . . and celebrate with them. In time, it's miraculous. It's the best evangelism. Go and get the kids there, but celebrate and be present with who is there. Don't worry about who is not. In time, they'll come.

Adult Leader

Animating youth ministry in the parish also includes the important work of advocating for young people's roles within parish organizations and the parish community as a whole. Effective coordinators know that sometimes they have to sell youth ministry to a parish community that might not know or understand the giftedness of youth.

We look at young people and we see God. We see a reflection of God. But so many people don't. So our job is to go out there and make sure that people know that. We're advocates.

Adult Leader

The youth minister is the bridge between the youth and the adult so you need them to be advocating for you, not just arguing why you can't do things.

Youth Participant

Going beyond the parish boundaries enhances youth ministry, and effective coordinators know how to network with others to expand their ministry efforts. Staying connected to the diocese, parishes in their community, and national opportunities is important. Through these connections, parishes are able to offer ministry opportunities that go beyond what one parish could offer.

Our youth minister is good at making connections, networking among other parishes and dioceses and other dioceses at the national level.

Parish Staff

Adult leaders also speak about the importance of networking with other coordinators for support, ideas, and help in times of crisis. New coordinators, in particular, need the wisdom and example that can be found in others who are experienced, but all appreciate being able to have someone to share stories and ideas with.

> What gives me hope? All of you. All of you here—deeply faith-filled, committed people. You have a wonderful sense of humor. The reason is because of the good news. You have to be committed to that. All of you give me hope.
>
> *Adult Leader*

> You have to have networking. You have to have people that are in youth ministry that you can gripe to, just bounce things off of.
>
> *Adult Leader*

Adult Volunteers

Young people need trusted adults in their lives. Their age or marital status is not important to young people. What is important is that adults are present and open to young people.

Leadership Finding 4: The Qualities of Adult Volunteers

Adults who work with youth must be genuine and real. They must have a passion for youth and be faith-filled. They are willing to be present to youth where they are: in the context of their lives. These adult volunteers build positive relationships with young people that are based in faith.

Youth can spot a phony from a great distance. They know which adults are committed to them and which are just putting in time. Youth spoke with great passion about the adults who were involved in their youth ministry. If the adults are genuine and real, the youth respond.

> They have such a commitment to you. They have a job and have a life and have their own children. They have their own life and then they are committed to you. It is a great comfort.
>
> *Youth Participant*

I guess it probably goes without saying—they have to really love the youth. You have to love youth, their music, their way of dressing, their way of speaking, their own little culture. You have to know and appreciate and respect that.

Parish Staff

You have to be yourself—with all your little flaws and everything else. And they love your flaws.

Parish Staff

Adults also must be able to share their story, which means, in part, being comfortable enough in their own skin to share their real self with another. Young people are looking for adults who will share their wisdom but are not afraid to let the young people struggle a little too. As one youth eloquently stated:

I am just saying that there's a large part of the time when the adults are older and wiser than we are and they have the benefit of the years of going through the same questions that we did. But I think what is so important is that we go through the questioning and we talk it out without immediately being told we're wrong.

Youth Participant

Young people need to experience faithful adults in order for them to understand what faith lived out looks like. Adults themselves must be on a journey of faith if they are going to be able to accompany a young person on his or her journey.

Young people have those core people who are in their own parish community that they have relied on. They've seen them witness of their own faith.

Adult Leader

In our parish youth ministry it is not just about the kids, but it's also about kids interacting with the adults in the parish and learning—the kids learning from the adults and the adults learning from the kids.

Youth Participant

Adults who work effectively with youth know how to connect to youth who are struggling and exploring questions. They accept immaturity, incessant questions, and other youthful behavior. Effective parishes take outreach ministry seriously and spend time going out to the places where young people are, to be present to them and to invite them into parish involvement.

> Our youth ministry comes from us walking the streets and inviting people to come and participate.
>
> *Adult Leader*

> You need to go where they are before you can get them to come to where you want them to be. You can't stand on the street and holler that you have something great over here unless you go over to their side of the street and see where they are at; to be present, and then that gives ideas on how to make them be present on your side of the street.
>
> *Parish Staff*

Training and Formation

Adults, both coordinators and volunteers, need formation and training for their roles. Effective parishes are intentional about providing training, matching people to the right jobs, and being attentive to the faith lives of adults.

"Leadership development . . . develops and nurtures adult leaders of lively faith and maturity with solid theological understandings, relational and ministry skills, and organizational ability appropriate to their particular role in ministry with adolescents."

(USCCB, RTV, p. 41)

Leadership Finding 5: The Importance of Training

Training and formation is important for adults working in youth ministry. Adult leaders need to grow in their faith and learn skills for ministry. It is important to match the gifts and talents of adults to the right roles in youth ministry.

Effective parishes do not assume that adults automatically will be good at working with youth. Effective coordinators learn the skill of assessing the gifts of their volunteers and then work hard to match them to the right roles. They make sure that the volunteer gets the training and support necessary to succeed at the job they have been given. Effective coordinators know that if volunteers have a positive experience and feel good about their contributions they will most likely volunteer again.

> We made a concerted effort about a year and a half ago to really put money and time into forming volunteers. That would be a huge focus for us. It made a whole lot of difference.
>
> *Adult Leader*

> I find the more prepared people are in general, the more likely that you'll get them to come back and you'll have a fulfilling experience as opposed to when you just throw them in there. They're like, "What am I doing?" They want to know specifically what is going to be asked of them and then train them to do it.
>
> *Parish Staff*

In addition to practical skills, all of those who work in ministry with youth also need spiritual development. This came out as a very strong recommendation from the research symposium. The parish youth ministry leaders attending the symposium were adamant about the importance of spiritual formation for themselves and their volunteers. This was also evident in the research when youth talked about the qualities of the adults who work in youth ministry and the kinds of faith formation or catechesis that they felt was effective. Youth are looking for inspiration and spiritual authenticity in the leaders who share faith.

Pastors, Parish Staffs, and Youth as Leaders

Three other groups play an essential role in youth ministry leadership at effective parishes: pastors, parish staffs, and youth. Without the combined leadership of these groups, parishes struggle to provide effective ministry to youth. The importance of these groups is explored in chapters 1 and 2 of this book.

Recommendations

Leadership is a learned skill. Parishes with effective youth ministry have ministers who can inspire others, mentor new leaders, and know the importance of leading from a vision. To enhance the leadership for youth ministry at your parish, consider the following eight implications.

1: Youth ministry leaders must nurture their spirituality. Youth ministry leaders should find prayer styles that help them grow in faith. They should be intentional about creating time and space for spiritual reflection. Other opportunities for spiritual enrichment are attending Mass, finding a spiritual director, and praying for their ministry with others. All of these are ways that they can continue to experience God's presence in their life and reflect on the Good News.

2: Coordinators should network with other coordinators of youth ministry. We all need support and help along the way, and no one knows the struggles of youth ministry better than those engaged in the ministry. New coordinators can find a mentor who will help to guide their work and support them as they learn more about the ministry. They can work with other youth ministers on local or diocesan projects. Beware of isolation. Adults in ministry need a community of peers as much as the young people do.

3: Utilize local and national resources for developing responsive youth ministry. Diocesan offices and national organizations have resources, information, and training that can enhance your ministry. Pay attention to what is being offered and make good decisions about what will benefit you, your volunteers, and the young people of the parish. National and international events offer young people a profound experience of the larger church and help to inspire faith. Nationally sponsored or diocesan service weeks, leadership programs, and retreats offer opportunities for young people that may not be available locally.

4: Develop a coordinating team of youth and adults to vision and plan for effective youth ministry. The coordinating team helps to shape the vision and direction for the ministry and direct youth ministry programs. The adults on the team have a unique opportunity to build meaningful relationships to youth. The youth on the team serve as peer leaders and inspire the participation and leadership growth of their peers.

5: Nurture the skills and the spirituality of the adults who work with youth in your parish. Provide ongoing training opportunities for your adult leaders. Mentor adults into new leadership roles. Host an adult retreat each year for your volunteers. Give adult leaders specific feedback about their ministry efforts. Pray all the time. All of these options help the adults who work with your young people to grow in their own faith and to learn the skills necessary for effective youth ministry.

6: Involve youth in leadership, ministry, and teaching roles in youth ministry and in the parish. Young people can transform your parish and your youth ministry efforts when they are allowed to make a difference. As one coordinator told us: "I told my kids once, don't bring me problems, bring me solutions; and it's amazing some of the solutions they'll come up with. Some that I would have never thought of or attempted, but they said, 'Let's do this one.'" Create leadership roles within youth ministry and within the parish. Make sure that young people get the training and support that they need to succeed. Tomorrow's Present, a research project on Catholic youth leadership, showed that young people who were involved in parish leadership as youth went on to value parish leadership and involvement as adults. Your investment in youth now can have a profound effect on the leadership of the church in the future.

7: Coordinators of youth ministry need to take the time to develop their skills. Your parish coordinator of youth ministry cannot be expected to know everything! But they can be expected to provide the leadership that your parish needs. To do that effectively, coordinators may need to study, reflect, establish a vision, and trust in others to help them. Coordinators must be intentional about learning what they do not currently know—through diocesan training programs, certificate training programs, college and seminary programs, and mentoring programs.

8: Coordinators of youth ministry should be intentional about their relationship to their pastor, the parish staff, and the parish community. Coordinators must be in relationship with the other leaders of the parish if they are going to help infuse young people into the parish and to engage the adults in ministering to the parish. They can do this by finding projects that can build cross-ministry relationships. They can invite other parish organizations to collaborate with them. They can be the pastor's and parish staff's public relations person.

Conclusion

During the youth interviews, it was sometimes obvious that effective, healthy, loving adults worked with the young people. And this was most obvious when they were not actually talking about the adults. They would be sharing a story about their own personal faith journey, and it would become apparent that they had a trusted adult who accompanied them. One young person told a story about discovering her own style of leadership, which led the researchers to wonder: Who was the adult who helped her name this? Youth talked about the importance of doing service and how much they learned by reflecting on their call to justice—leading to the question, "Who was leading the reflection?"

Parishes with effective youth ministry love young people. This usually begins at the top. The pastor and parish staffs that were interviewed for this project have such passion for young people. They spoke with emotion about watching youth grow in leadership and faith. They are passionate about creating more and more ways that the whole parish could minister to the young people. These parishes also have qualified, educated, self-directed coordinators who take their call to ministry very seriously. These coordinators are grounded in a vision for youth ministry that includes all the youth of the parish. They know how important it is to engage the gifts of other adults. They know, ultimately, that the Body of Christ is bigger than they are and that if they do not engage other adults in ministering to youth, the young people will suffer.

Assessment Questions

When working with the parish staff, leadership groups, and the leadership team for youth ministry, consider the following questions in assessing your community.

For Coordinators of Youth Ministry

- How do I take the time to nurture my spirituality and skills for ministry?

- How do I develop collaborative relationships with parish staff and leaders?

- In what ways do I advocate for youth and their involvement in parish life?

- In what ways do I network with other youth ministers and with the diocese?

- How do I make youth and adults feel invited, welcome, and comfortable?

Regarding Adult Volunteers

- How does our community invite and nurture adults with lively faith to work with youth?

- How do we provide training and formation for adult volunteers who work with youth?

CHAPTER 5

Developing Effective Practices of Dynamic Youth Ministry

The many voices that come together in this research project share good news for people who care about youth and want them to grow as young disciples and belong deeply within the community of faith. The good news is that youth ministry works when parishes embrace their young people, provide strong leadership, and offer appropriate activities. In the parishes with effective youth ministry, the factors identified in previous chapters come together to help the parish embrace, include, and empower young disciples.

In the introduction, the findings describe the impact of youth ministry in transforming the life of a young person and the life of the parish community. The first chapter highlights the importance of parish support for youth ministry. This support springs from understanding and common vision among pastor, parish staff, and the wider parish. The second chapter describes the qualities and dimensions of youth ministry. This section describes variety, hospitality, and innovation as marks of effective youth ministry. Youth ownership and partnership with families also distinguishes youth ministry efforts in these parishes.

The third chapter points to high-impact elements within a youth ministry program. Faith formation is described as the heart of youth ministry. Extended trips, retreats, and service projects are noted for their impact on youth and the way these events build community. Youth involvement in liturgy as members of the assembly and in the ministries has tremendous impact on youth and the community. The fourth chapter explains the role that effective leadership plays in parishes with dynamic youth ministry. The attitudes, actions, and qualities of the coordinator of youth ministry are highlighted, and the image of animator is suggested as a way to understand this empowering leadership style. The openness and faithfulness of all adults who work with youth is identified as a critical element for effective youth ministry.

Research Themes

Some of the observations of the research team and the symposium participants go beyond these categories that address the individual findings. They identified themes to help to describe the overall portrait of youth ministry within the ninety-six parish communities that participated in this research. For example, in the introduction, the theme of the willing parish is identified. Four additional themes emerge from the research in describing effective youth ministry.

The Importance of Spirituality

One important theme that emerged is the importance of spirituality in youth ministry. This has two dimensions—first, the spirituality of adults who work with youth; and second, attention to spirituality within youth ministry gatherings and strategies.

Youth who engage with adults of vibrant faith grow as disciples and Christian leaders. They are looking for adults who have authentic faith and genuine compassion. Young people expect this sincerity and are disillusioned when they do not find adults living lives of faith boldly and consistently. When they do encounter authentic disciples, they want to stay, learn, grow, and share their own experience. Thus, for leaders who work with youth, a deep spirituality is the cornerstone from which the ministry must flow. Furthermore, adult youth ministry leaders

> **"**Part of the vision of youth ministry is to present to youth the richness of the person of Christ, which perhaps exceeds the ability of one person to capture, but which might be effected by the collective ministry of the many persons who make up the church.**"**
>
> (The USCCB Department of Education, A Vision of Youth Ministry, p. 24)

consistently described how nurturing their spiritual life is essential for their longevity in the ministry.

Spirituality is also central to the events, gatherings, and strategies of a parish's ministry with youth. Prayer, faith formation, inspiration, and witness are essential to effective youth ministry. Without this focus, gatherings and activities can be reduced to recreation.

Experience of Community

A second theme concerns belonging within a community. Youth ministry is most effective when youth experience community; this experience of belonging makes many more aspects of formation and ministry possible. In community, youth experience the body of Christ in their midst. They understand the good news in new ways because the Christian message is embodied within the community. Youth are seeking a meaningful experience of community. This experience is not common in our society in general because of the prevalence of many distractions and barriers to community.

This research project indicates a strong correlation between the vibrancy of parish life in general and the effectiveness of youth ministry. In general, the parishes that were studied had a vibrant overall parish life, and the youth ministry reflected the general dynamism of the parish's ministries and the collaborative environment of the parish staff and leadership. Given these factors, the research team identified that the starting point for growing youth ministry is different depending upon the vibrancy of parish life. This implies different strategies for parishes at different levels of parish life development.

Consider Figure 5-1. Parishes are divided into four quadrants based upon the vibrancy of parish life and the effectiveness of youth ministry. The first quadrant represents parishes with underdeveloped parish ministry and underdeveloped youth ministry. The second quadrant includes parishes with effective youth ministry but developing underdeveloped parish ministry overall. The third quadrant represents parishes with vibrant parish ministry but developing youth ministry. The fourth quadrant includes communities that have vibrant parish ministry and effective youth ministry.

Parishes that need to develop effective youth ministry can have different starting points depending upon whether they identify with quadrant 1 or quadrant 3. A parish that has vibrant ministry overall (quadrant 3) should seek first to link youth to the life of the parish, then develop opportunities for

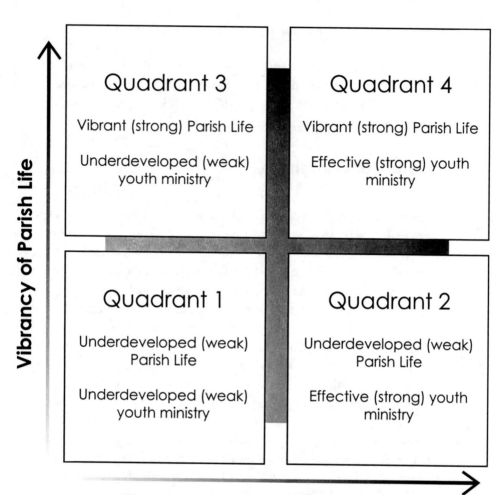

Vibrancy of Parish Life (vertical axis)

Quadrant 3	Quadrant 4
Vibrant (strong) Parish Life Underdeveloped (weak) youth ministry	Vibrant (strong) Parish Life Effective (strong) youth ministry
Quadrant 1	Quadrant 2
Underdeveloped (weak) Parish Life Underdeveloped (weak) youth ministry	Underdeveloped (weak) Parish Life Effective (strong) youth ministry

Effectiveness of Youth Ministry (horizontal axis)

Figure 5–1

youth to be ministered to through specific youth-focused activities that complement their involvement in general parish life.

In parishes where the overall parish life is in need of development (quadrant 1), youth ministry has more of a need to create community, faith formation, worship, and service opportunities for youth through youth-focused activities. In a sense, in parishes where youth do not experience the parish community to be an example of a vibrant community of disciples, this experience needs to be developed within youth ministry. In these parishes, youth and youth ministry may be an energizing factor in helping to develop more vibrant ministries overall.

This has profound implications for all who support parishes in developing effective youth ministry. Diocesan leaders, training organizations, publishers, and national organizations need to respond to parishes differently, depending upon the overall health of parish life. Suggestions that work for some parishes would only lead to frustration and futility in others. For instance, in a parish that has weak and dreary worship, it isn't helpful to simply tell youth ministry leaders to include youth in the liturgical ministries. Youth should have experiences of vibrant worship in order to experience the call and formation for liturgical ministry involvement. In a parish that has dysfunctional and contentious leadership dynamics, it isn't helpful or fair to suggest that youth be placed on the parish council.

The good news here is that every parish can find a place to start. There is not a perfect, one-size-fits-all remedy or starting point for all parishes. Some leaders can feel like they are pushing a two-ton rock up a large hill because they are trying to implement youth ministry in a way that mimics the parish next door. Youth ministry is deeply relational and personal. Each parish can learn from other parishes' experiences, but each community needs to find its own way to effective ministry with youth.

A Comprehensive Vision for Youth Ministry

A third theme compares the findings from these parishes with the vision for Catholic youth ministry. At the national symposium, leaders compared the findings from these parishes with the vision of youth ministry outlined in *Renewing the Vision*. Symposium participants found the research results to be very affirming of *Renewing the Vision*, especially the comprehensive approach to ministry and the integration of youth within parish life.

The parishes in the research implemented the principles of this document in different ways, oftentimes organizing a variety of ministry initiatives around a primary ministry effort such as a youth community or sacramental preparation. Some components of the vision such as evangelization and pastoral care were not found to be as prevalent in the research as they are envisioned in *Renewing the Vision*. Symposium participants suggested that the need for the spiritual formation of leaders was more evident in the research than in *Renewing the Vision* and that this emphasis would complement the continued development of youth ministry.

Elements of a Youth Ministry Program Model

A fourth theme concerns the development of a program model for youth ministry. As was stated in the introduction, the parishes in this research do not have one common program model, but most of these effective parishes have elements in common that seem to work in concert to develop effective youth ministry. These parishes pay attention to the following elements in developing their youth ministry approach.

Provide a pattern for gathering with youth on a regular basis. These regular gatherings can be weekly, biweekly, or monthly. Because youth can count on these gatherings, a community can be nurtured and developed. Parents can also actively encourage participation because it becomes part of the family pattern.

Provide special events and ways to gather with youth. These events are all the gatherings of youth that aren't part of the regular pattern. This would include day-long service events, Friday night socials, retreats, trips, youth conventions, open-gym night, and a variety of ways for youth to get together with caring adults. These offerings round out the youth ministry program and provide ways for youth with different interests to participate. The extended trips, retreats, and service experiences provide a means for greater personal conversion and stronger community.

Develop intentional methods for providing adolescent catechesis. Adolescent catechesis includes both the informal, teachable moments within youth ministry and the inten-

> **"**The comprehensive approach is not a single program or recipe for ministry. Rather, it provides a way for integrating ministry with adolescents and their families into the total life and mission of the Church, recognizing that the whole community is responsible for this ministry.**"**
>
> (USCCB, RTV, p. 19)

tional faith learning, accomplished through a variety of ways. Some parishes infuse a curriculum for faith growth throughout youth ministry. Some parishes provide faith formation for youth within events and programs with the whole parish community in an intergenerational model. Other parishes provide religious education and sacramental preparation as a distinct element of youth ministry. The important common factor is that effective parishes *plan* for faith formation for adolescents as an intentional part of their model.

Develop opportunities for youth who want to grow deeper in faith. Some youth are looking for a community to belong to and a chance to socialize with other youth. But other youth are looking for a way to learn and grow in their faith by going deeper into issues of discipleship and conversion. These youth can become annoyed and distracted by youth who do not want to be there. If they feel that youth ministry is just social or that teaching is watered down, they will go elsewhere. Effective parishes provide opportunities for these youth to go deeper in their faith with knowledgeable adults and other like-minded peers.

Provide non-gathered ways to connect with youth. There are a lot of ways to minister with youth without having them come to the parish or to an event. This would include sending things to youth: e-mail prayers and greetings, birthday cards, study kits, newsletters, prayer cards, emergency phone number cards, and other resources. This also includes being present to youth where they are. For example, youth ministry team members can attend sporting events or concerts in which youth are participating.

Connect youth to the life of the parish. Youth are ministered to as part of parish life. Through the variety of components of the parish's ministry, youth experience ministry side by side with adults and children. Many parish events become a youth ministry strategy when you are intentional in making sure that youth are included in the prayers, stories, examples, and teaching of the event. For example, the parish mission can be part of the youth ministry's Lenten preparations if you take the time to prepare the mission speaker to speak to youth in the assembly.

Provide ways to connect with families. Begin by communicating with parents about youth ministry and by considering the impact of youth ministry on families as you plan. Strengthen family life by providing parents of adolescents with helpful programs and resources and by providing occasional gatherings for families of adolescents.

Provide ways for youth to be involved in ministry, leadership, and service. Besides being ministered to, youth desire a way to share their gifts; they long for a chance to serve. An effective model for youth ministry will include ways to encourage youth to be involved in liturgical and catechetical ministries, in leadership for youth ministry, by sharing leadership in the parish, and by involvement in community service.

Developing Effective Youth Ministry Practices

Where do you start if you are someone who cares about youth and wants effective youth ministry? This book includes recommendations for strategies that could help parishes implement these findings in practical and specific ways. To become more effective in youth ministry, consider these overall starting points.

1: Begin with prayer. Youth Ministry is a vital part of your parish's mission. Mission begins with prayer. Pray for youth in your community, for parents of youth, for youth leaders, and for youth ministry events and strategies. Pray that youth ministry in your parish guides youth to be disciples of Jesus Christ and active members of the faith community.

66 *By offering this framework, we seek to provide direction to the church's ministry and to affirm and encourage local creativity.* 99

(USCCB, RTV, p. 20)

66 *Because major change is so difficult to accomplish, a powerful force is required to sustain the process.* 99

(John P. Kotter, Leading Change, p. 51)

2: Build a guiding coalition. A guiding coalition for youth ministry is a team of people in your parish who have enough authority and commitment to guide the development of more effective youth ministry. A guiding coalition moves the community from an overreliance on one individual leader. This coalition is also not a weak committee that works hard but ultimately has no influence in effecting change. A strong guiding coalition should include parish staff and key leaders as it guides your parish through assessment, visioning, and planning for more effective youth ministry.

3: Assess your current youth ministry effectiveness. Two tools in this book can help your parish team assess the qualities and elements in your youth ministry efforts. To identify the elements in your model for youth ministry, use the list in this chapter under the section heading, "Elements of a Youth Ministry Program Model." For each of these elements, ask the question: "How does our community provide for this element of youth ministry?" To identify your parish's strengths and weaknesses in terms of qualities, attitudes, specific program elements, and leadership, use the assessment questions at the end of chapters 1 through 4.

4: Have a vision for your parish youth ministry. Take the time as a parish to name your vision and goals for youth ministry. Use *Renewing the Vision* as your starting point. Compare this vision to your assessment of youth ministry to guide your planning for future effectiveness.

5: Listen to youth, their parents, parish staff, and leadership, including the leaders who work with youth. In this research project, the youth, adult leaders, and parish staff members were ready and anxious to talk about youth ministry and what was working and what wasn't. Adapt and utilize some of the questions in appendix A that were used in the research interviews to listen to youth, parents, parish staff, and the leaders who work with youth.

6: Invest time and resources. In *Renewing the Vision*, parishes are urged to support youth with "prayer, time, facilities and money." To be effective in youth ministry, communities need to make these efforts a pastoral priority. Effective youth ministry is not a quick-fix. To become effective, it will take resources, and it will take time to grow.

7: Develop a model that fits your parish. Effective parishes put youth ministry together in a way that matches their community, their youth, their resources, and their personality. Use the elements listed in the heading "Elements of a Youth Ministry Program Model" as a guide to build your model for parish youth ministry.

8: Evaluate and innovate. Effective parishes are guided by their relationship to youth and their families. By knowing young people, they create responsive ministry. Continually evaluate youth ministry programs and strategies based upon what is working in your community. Your evaluation and your vision for youth ministry can inspire innovative ways to serve and include youth.

Conclusion

The research team used the image of a conversation to describe this research process for identifying effective practices in Catholic youth ministry. Conversations have no predetermined ending or outcome; they continue as long as people have energy for the topic and remain engaged in the dialogue. We hope that this research begins or energizes a local conversation in your parish about how to serve, include, and empower young disciples. All parishes have room to grow and faithful ministry to celebrate. We hope that your community can find itself in this description of effective youth ministry and that these factors and elements can be helpful in guiding the development of youth ministry. As this critical dialogue continues, may the faithfulness, creativity, and commitment in your community become part of the shared story of dynamic youth ministry.

Additional research findings and support can be found at *www.cmdnet.org/ dynamicyouthministry*. Comments and questions can also be directed to one of the e-mail addresses provided on the Contact page on the site.

Description of Research Process

The *Effective Youth Ministry Practices in Catholic Parishes* project was designed to help parishes strengthen their youth ministry. What the research team wanted to accomplish was to provide a document that would put parishes that want to create or strengthen their youth ministry "in the room" with parishes that have already developed effective, dynamic ministry with adolescents. This document would give parishes who are seeking guidance models to emulate, characteristics to nurture, and practices to adapt.

To research effective youth ministry practices in Catholic parishes, the research team utilized a qualitative research method. In their book *Beginning Qualitative Research*, Pam Maykut and Richard Morehouse (who also served as consultants for the effective practices project) describe this research method. Qualitative research is a research model that "examines people's words and action in narrative or descriptive ways more closely representing the situation as experienced by the participants" (p. 2).

To accomplish the aims of the project, the subject of the research was the *practices* of effective youth ministry. Practices include a wide variety of behaviors, attitudes, and disciplines. A practice has within it personal and communal values, beliefs, and convictions. In other words, practices are beliefs that take flesh in actions and choices. A focus on practices means that we asked parishes to tell us what they do with youth and to describe the "practice" of how youth are part of parish life.

Another research factor was the focus upon *best* practices. This project is not trying to portray a "state of the ministry" or a portrait of what is typically happening in parishes. The research was designed to study effective practices so parishes seeking to enhance their ministry will have models and examples to follow. The research team was careful not to limit the sample of parishes to those that fit any predetermined ideas about effectiveness. "Effective" was not defined by the research team but was determined by the diocesan hosts who arranged for parishes to be interviewed. Sites were identified based upon various diversity factors. Diocesan hosts were instructed to choose adult leaders, youth, and parish staffs from communities considered to be providing effective youth ministry.

Interview Site Selection

To listen to and experience effective practices in these parishes, the research team conducted forty-nine interviews in thirteen sites across the United States. Some of these sites were a single diocese and some represented a regional cluster of dioceses. These sites were chosen based upon:

- Geographical diversity—A representation of regions across the nation

- Availability of diversity of urban, suburban, and rural parishes.

Within each site, leaders from eight to ten parishes were interviewed. This included a group interview with adult leaders from each of the parishes, a group interview with youth from each of the parishes, and on-site interviews of parish staffs at two of the parishes.

The criteria for being part of the adult leader interview were that the person should be an adult and should have over one year of experience in working with youth in the parish. Most of the adult leaders were parish coordinators of youth ministry, but volunteer adult leaders were also included. This group is identified as "adult leaders" rather than just "leaders" because many of the youth interviewed were leaders as well.

The diocesan hosts were asked to select parishes based upon the following diversity factors:

- Diversity of urban, suburban, and rural

- Ethnic and racial diversity

- Diversity in styles and methods of youth ministry

- Diversity of leadership: full-time paid, part-time paid, and volunteer coordinators of youth ministry.

Based on these criteria, ninety-six parishes were selected to participate in the adult leader and youth group interviews, and twenty-three parishes were chosen for the on-site staff interviews. The hosts in the larger urban areas included parishes that minister primarily to Hispanic and African American youth.

Research Method Factors

The research team considered the following factors in setting up the research process.

1: Choosing a focus of inquiry. A focus of inquiry is the primary statement of purpose that determines much of the research process. The research team determined this to be our focus of inquiry: *We want to understand more about the experiences and views of youth, adult ministers, and parish staff on youth ministry.*

2: Sampling strategy. The sampling strategy employed in this project was a combination of two purposeful sampling strategies. The first strategy is called intensity sampling and is also referred to as a "best practices" nomination approach. This strategy considers information-rich cases that manifest the phenomenon intensely, but not extremely, such as studying good students or poor students.[1] In this project, the intensity sampling was determined by focusing on parishes identified as having "effective youth ministry."

The second sampling strategy is called maximum variation sampling. Its purpose is to document unique or diverse variations that have emerged in adapting to different conditions. It identifies important common patterns that cut across variations.[2] For this project, the maximum variation sampling occurred as a result of the intended diversity factors that are listed above.

3: Resulting sample characteristics. There were a total of ninety-six parishes who participated in the interviews. Tables A–1, A–2, A–3, and A–4 indicate the diverse makeup of the interview sites and groups.

Table A–1 Regional Diversity for the 13 Diocesan Sites

Sites	Region
3	Northeast and Mid-Atlantic
3	Midwest
2	Southeast
1	Texas
2	Mountain States
2	West Coast

Table A–2 Parish Information

Demographics

18 parishes described themselves as Rural
47 parishes described themselves as Suburban
24 parishes described themselves as Urban
 7 parishes were undescribed

Average Income of Families in Parishes

# of Parishes	Average Family Income
8	$15,000 to $25,000
22	$26,000 to $36,000
17	$37,000 to $47,000
20	$48,000 to $60,000
13	over $60,000
16	income not reported

Parish Size

Parishes ranged in size from 125 families to 6,200 families.

# of Parishes	# of Families
9	125 to 349
12	350 to 999
11	1,000 to 1,499
12	1,500 to 1,999
19	2,000 to 2,999
14	3,000 +
19	did not report

Staff for Youth Ministry in Parish

# of Full-Time Positions	# of Parishes
0	31
1	29
2	18
3	2
4	3
more than 4	1
did not report	12

Table A–3 Youth Statistics

The total number of youth interviewed was 140.

Age of Youth

# of Youth	Ages
1	14
17	15
32	16
58	17
23	18
4	19
5	did not report

Gender

91	Female
49	Male

Ethnicity of Youth

# of Youth	Ethnic Identification
10	African American
3	Asian American
100	European American
12	Latino
3	Native American
11	other
8	not reporting ethnicity

Schools Attended by Youth

Youth	Type of School
30	Catholic school
4	other private school
98	public school
2	other
8	did not report

Table A–4 Adults Who Were Interviewed

The total number of adults interviewed was 232, as part of the adult leader interviews and the parish staff interviews.

Gender

133	Female
82	Male
17	did not report

Ethnicity

# of Adults	Ethnic Identification
4	African American
1	Asian American
105	European American
5	Latino
5	Native American
2	other
110	not reporting ethnicity

4: Method of data collection. The data was collected through group interviews conducted by the research team. For each of the interviews, members of the research team were sent off in pairs, one man and one woman. Each pair conducted the interviews for two sites in one trip. For the adult leader and youth interviews, the two groups were gathered together for hospitality, introductions, and prayer. When the groups were divided, one interviewer went with each group. Each group answered the questions as provided in the interview guide for that constituency (youth or adult leader). The interviews lasted from 90 to 120 minutes. Each interview was tape-recorded, and the sessions began with participants providing permission to be taped and assuming an alias for the interview time to protect their privacy.

The parish staff interviews were similar, although sometimes, by necessity, they were shorter. The parish coordinator of youth ministry did not usually participate in the interview since they had already provided their input. Additionally, the adult leader did not participate so that the parish staff wouldn't over-rely upon the "youth minister" to answer the questions and so that the staff would speak freely about youth ministry in the parish. For the parish staff interviews, the participants included pastors, directors of religious education, pastoral ministers, liturgy coordinators, Christian outreach and service coordinators, bookkeepers, support staff, and many others.

A total of forty-nine group interviews were conducted in the thirteen sites, as follows:

- 13 groups of adult leaders in youth ministry

- 13 groups of youth

- 23 groups of parish staff

To conduct the interviews, sets of interview questions were created and used as guides for the group interviews.

Adult Interview Questions

- What is youth ministry in your parish?

- You've all been involved for some time with youth ministry. Tell us about a really meaningful experience.

- In youth ministry at your parish, what's worked?

- How do you know it's worked?

- What hasn't worked?

- How do you know it hasn't worked?

- What are the features of a healthy, thriving youth ministry?

- What helps this happen?

- What are the barriers to this?

(Two options for closing question)

- How has your involvement in youth ministry helped you to grow in your relationship with God? OR

- What gives you hope?

Youth Interview Questions

- What is youth ministry in your parish?

- Tell us about an experience of being involved in youth ministry that was really meaningful to you.

- Tell us about an experience that has helped you grow in your relationship to God.

- In youth ministry at your parish, what's worked?

- How do you know it's worked?

- In any parish, some youth choose to participate in youth ministry and some don't. When youth choose not to get involved in youth ministry, why do you think they make that choice?

- What makes for a really good youth ministry?

- What helps this happen?

- What gets in the way?

- What gives you hope?

Parish Staff Interview Questions

- What is youth ministry in your parish?

- You are all involved in this parish in a variety of ways and you see the interactions between youth and the parish from different perspectives. Tell us about a meaningful experience of youth being involved in ministry in your community.

- In youth ministry at your parish, what's worked?

- How do you know it's worked?

- What hasn't worked?

- How do you know it hasn't worked?

- What are the features of a healthy, thriving youth ministry?

- What helps this happen?

- What are the barriers to this?

- What gives you hope?

5: Preparation for data analysis. Each of the forty-nine interviews was transcribed from the tapes. These transcripts formed the basis of the research compilation. The full transcripts were coded to identify the group interview site and group. These transcripts were then duplicated for the data analysis. To prepare for the data analysis, each member of the research team read the transcripts of the interviews that she or he conducted.

6: Data analysis. To analyze the data, the research team "unitized" the data (isolating parts of the transcripts that focused on a particular theme or topic). The research team divided into three teams to analyze the data: youth, adult leaders, and parish staff. Each team read all of the transcripts for their constituency and then began the process of sorting the data and arriving at the outcomes or findings. Throughout the process of data analysis, the team tried to stay close to the data so that the voices of the people interviewed were truly honored and respected.

The units of data were then analyzed and were grouped by the topics they addressed to determine the key findings (see Appendix B for key findings for each constituency group). The teams worked to identify the most important findings and then to identify other findings that were related to or supportive of these key findings. Additional findings that were not related to the key findings were left to stand on their own. All together there were 121 findings, as follows:

- 40 youth findings

- 40 adult leader findings

- 41 parish staff findings

There seems to be more convergence than divergence among the findings: We described it as views of the same mountain from three different sides. It was not like the story of the blind men describing the elephant where each describes its part as the whole; in this case, all three groups had a sense of the whole conversation, but in expressing what they felt was important, each kept their own voice and perspective.

The findings of the data analysis for the three groups were then analyzed together to determine the key findings for all three groups that are reported in this book. There were sixteen findings that emerged.

7: Provisions for trustworthiness. The following were identified as the provisions for trustworthiness utilized within this research process:

- Detailed description of the research process and outcomes

- Using a team process

- Including peer debriefers (the research consultants)

- Development of an audit trail so that all information can be traced back to original interview transcript

Symposium

After the initial data analysis was completed, a symposium was held to further the research and explore implications for the field of Catholic youth ministry. The fifty-five people attending the symposium included diocesan youth ministry leaders, parish youth ministry leaders, and leaders from organizations involved in supporting youth ministry, such as publishers, training organizations, and national organizations. One of the processes that was conducted during the symposium was an exploration of the themes that emerged from the key findings in the research. Each group explored the implications and the observable practices as identified in the findings and participant quotations. The discussions of this gathering assisted the research team in refining the research findings and preparing for the identification of the overall findings.

1. Patton, M. Q. (1990). *Qualitative Evaluation and Research Methods* (2nd Edition). Newbury Park, CA: Sage. Table 5.5: Sampling Strategies.
2. Ibid.

Research Findings by Constituency Group

A constituency group is a grouping of interviews in which the participants have a common interest or perspective on the subject. Each group is an important source of data within the research project. The data collected for each group is analyzed separately in order to preserve the "voice" of these participants in the research. The findings in this book were a combination of the findings from the three groups that were interviewed: youth, adult leaders in youth ministry, and parish staff members. Below you will find the twelve most significant findings from the interviews with each group.

Youth Interviews

The following list represents the twelve most significant findings from the interviews with youth.

Vibrant liturgy. Vibrant liturgy engages youth in an experience that touches their mind, body, and heart; connects youth more deeply with community; and strengthens their faith.

Retreats. Retreats (including mandatory ones) often serve as an entry point leading to deeper relationships with God and others.

Service. Christian service experiences significantly impact young people's relationship with God. These experiences change their perspective on life by increasing their awareness that they are doing more than just service; they are doing God's work.

Youth leadership. Leadership experiences benefit young people by providing them with opportunities to explore various leadership roles and styles, both with their peers and with the adult church community.

Reasons for not participating in youth ministry. Fear of not being accepted, impressions of exclusivity, lack of time, issues of trust, cynicism about religion, misconceptions about church, and a history of bad experiences with religious education or youth programming are all reasons why young people choose not to participate in parish youth ministry.

Support of parish. When parish communities provide young people with loving support, the parish becomes a second home to youth. This support and these relationships with members of the parish community are crucial to young people's involvement.

Youth ministry is responsive. To be effective, youth ministry needs to be responsive to young people; this response must be creative, organized, advertised, and consistent.

Connecting life and faith. Youth ministry is a bridge that connects the real life of young people to church and faith. Youth grow spiritually from the intentional faith conversations that are guided, safe, and meaningful.

Catholic identity. Youth are often energized by the distinctive qualities of being Catholic. They are passionate about explaining how and why it connects them more deeply to God.

Adult leaders. Open-minded, mature adults help young people explore their faith by providing direction and boundaries during programs and conversations.

Parents. Parents' faith and their involvement—or lack of it—in the Church have a big impact on young people. Parents with vibrant faith and parents who are involved in the parish pass this passion on to their sons and daughters. Sometimes, youth ministry involvement for their child is an impetus for a parent's increased Church involvement and faith growth.

Partnership between adults and youth. Effective youth ministry requires an active, friendly partnership between adults and youth.

Adult Youth Minister Interviews

The following represents the twelve most significant findings from the interviews with the adult youth ministry leaders.

Youth leadership. In parishes with effective youth ministry, young people have ownership for the ministry—particularly by taking leadership. Adult youth ministers encourage youth to take ownership, provide youth with leadership training, and then get out of the way.

Family. Effective youth ministers want to be parents' allies in the faith formation of teens. Youth ministers express frustration that parents feel inadequate or apathetic in taking on their role in the faith formation process.

Support from parish staff and structures. Parishes with effective youth ministry have pastors, parish staffs, and pastoral councils who support youth and have a clear and common vision of youth ministry. They are collaborative in their planning and programming, integrating youth into all aspects of parish life. Staffs are mutually supportive of each other.

Role of the coordinator of youth ministry. Effective youth ministers know the success of the program isn't dependent upon them. They recognize that they have both strengths and weaknesses; they aren't always in charge; and ultimately, youth ministry is the ongoing work of the Holy Spirit.

Extended programs. Trips, camps, and other extended programs are important because they provide opportunities for good prayer and liturgy, leadership development, small faith groups, fun, and excitement. They have a unique ability to build community among young people and between youth and adults.

Youth ministry connects young people to God. The ultimate goal of youth ministry is to connect young people to God through the Catholic faith. This is done through prayer, discipleship opportunities, evangelization, and by connecting the young people to Jesus Christ.

Youth ministry is challenging. Effective youth ministry challenges young people to take risks, develop talents, learn about faith and morals, and become better people. Youth ministers sometimes need to say the hard things and must challenge young people with the truths of the Catholic faith.

Importance of creating community. Effective youth ministry is very intentional about creating an atmosphere (physical and emotional) where young people have a sense of belonging and are accepted. Important elements include personal invitation, welcoming, building community, and building relationships.

Volunteer leadership and training. Effective youth ministry needs volunteer youth ministers and catechists who share responsibility for the parish's youth ministry. Effective volunteers are described as being genuine and authentic, having a passion for young people, and being able to share their faith. Coordinators of youth ministry work to ensure that the right people are in the right jobs and that their volunteers represent a spectrum of ages.

Faith formation. Effective youth ministry understands catechesis as an important component of youth ministry. Catechesis occurs in a variety of ways and settings, but youth learn best when they are experientially engaged in the topic. The more it looks and feels like school, the less they learn. Conflicting understandings and approaches between youth ministers and religious education directors are barriers to effective faith formation.

Liturgy. Good liturgy is a priority; it includes music that is contemporary and homilies that youth can relate to, and it includes youth as liturgical ministers. There are differing opinions on the value of "youth masses." Some parishes see them as opportunities for liturgy that reaches young people; other parishes are wary of segregating youth from the larger parish.

Youth integrated into the parish. Effective youth ministry helps teens become integrated into the full life of the parish community. The parish gives youth a voice and recognizes that youth ministry is everyone's responsibility.

Parish Staff Interviews

The following list represents the twelve most significant findings from the interviews with parish staffs.

Support for youth ministry. Youth Ministry thrives with support from the pastor, the staff, and the whole parish community.

Youth role within parish. In parishes with effective youth ministry, youth are both weavers of parish life and woven into the entire fabric of parish life—including decision-making roles.

Parish's relationship to youth. Parishes with effective youth ministry genuinely like and know youth and show their affection by welcoming them and their contributions, by affirming them, and by encouraging them. Youth feel at home and safe in these parishes.

Coordinator of youth ministry. The person of the coordinator of youth ministry is formed by a deep sense of vocation but also the attitude, "I'm not the show." They believe it is their role to call forth and empower the gifts in the community. They balance direct ministry to youth with the coordination of volunteer leaders to animate dynamic youth ministry.

Faith formation. Faith formation is at the core of youth ministry and aims to touch the hearts of youth and their families. In adolescence, faith formation happens differently. It involves youth in planning and teaching. It involves hospitality and openness to mystery. It is about real life for the long haul. It is about the "so what" questions young people ask so they can understand how doctrinal statements make a difference in everyday life.

Youth leading within the parish. Youth are willing, excited, passionate leaders in the parish. They share their gifts and energy as leaders in parish life and in ministry to their peers.

Effects of youth ministry. Effective youth ministry has a transforming effect for a lifetime. The ministry plants seeds that help youth grow into great people and leaders who are faith-filled, enthusiastic, mature change agents with a good moral compass, and who have the ability to face life's challenges.

Effects of service. Service changes young people's lives, sometimes radically, sometimes for life. Service alters their self-image and creates empathy.

Parent and family involvement. Effective youth ministry insists on and gives real opportunity for parent and family involvement.

Adults who work with youth. Youth are open to adults who are real, go where youth are, companion youth on their spiritual journeys, and build respectful relationships with young people.

Balance within youth ministry. Effective youth ministry balances the social, educational, formational, sacramental, and service dimensions. It is "permeable" and there are no boundaries between the dimensions.

Responsive youth ministry. Effective youth ministry doesn't begin with a model, but rather responds to the real lives, needs, and interests of young people in the community. The leadership creates ministry by experimenting, taking risks, and "trying again." They put the pieces together in a way that is responsive to youth.

Acknowledgments

Scripture quotations are taken from the New Revised Standard Version Bible: Catholic Edition, copyright © 1989, 1993, Division of Christian Education of the National Council of Churches of Christ in the United States of America. All rights reserved. Used with permission.

The quotations on pages 17, 20, 32, 34, 36, 38, 48, 54, 60, 62, 66, 78, and 80 are from *Renewing the Vision: A Framework for Catholic Youth Ministry*, by the United States Conference of Catholic Bishops (USCCB) (Washington, DC: USCCB, Inc., 1997), pages 13, 35, 22, 25, 20, 26, 19, 41, 25, 41, 19, and 20 respectively. Copyright © 1997 by the USCCB, Inc., Washington, DC. All rights reserved. Used with permission.

The explanation of the parish on page 16 is quoted from *Communities of Salt and Light: Reflections on the Social Mission of the Parish* by the USCCB (Washington, DC: USCCB, Inc., 1993), page 1. Copyright © 1994 by the USCCB, Inc., Washington, DC.

The quotes on pages 18 and 24 are from *A Message to Youth: Pathway to Hope* by the USCCB Committee on the Laity (Washington, DC: USCCB, Inc., 1994), page 3. Copyright © 1995 by the USCCB, Inc., Washington, DC.

The quote on the youth ministry model on page 20, "The One-Eared Mickey Mouse," is by Stuart Cummings-Bond, published in *Youthworker* 6 Fall 1989. Page 76. Copyright © 1989 by Salem Publishing/CCM Communications.

The quote on page 44 is from *General Directory for Catechesis,* by the USCCB (Washington, DC: USCCB, Inc., 1998), page 176. Copyright © 1997 by the Libreria Editrice Vaticana.

The comment about World Youth Day on page 46 is quoted from "Letter of Pope John Paul II to Cardinal Eduardo Francisco Pironio on the Occasion of the Seminar on World Youth Days Organized in Czestochowa May 8, 1996", at *www.vatican.va/holy_father/john_paul_ii/letters/1996/documents/hf_jp-ii_let_19960508_czestochowa-gmg_en.html*, accessed August 28, 2003.

The quote on page 50 is from *The Challenge of Catholic Youth Evangelization: Called to Be Witnesses and Storytellers* by The National Federation for

Catholic Youth Ministry, Inc. (Washington, DC, 1993), page 20. Copyright © 1993 by the National Federation for Catholic Youth Ministry, Inc.

The quote on page 52 is from *From Age to Age: The Challenge of Worship with Adolescents* by The National Federation for Catholic Youth Ministry, Inc. (Washington, DC, 1997), page 2. Copyright © 1997 by the National Federation for Catholic Youth Ministry, Inc.

The future of humanity comment on page 58 is quoted from *"Pastoral Constitution on the Church in the Modern World Gaudium Et Spes Promulgated by His Holiness, Pope Paul VI on* December 7, 1965", at *www.vatican.va/archive/hist_ councils/ii_vatican_council/documents/vat-ii_cons_19651207_gaudium-et-spes_en. html*, accessed September 11, 2003.

The excerpt on page 74 is quoted from *A Vision of Youth Ministry* by the USCCB Department of Education (Washington, DC, 1986), page 24. Copyright © 1986 by the USCCB, Inc., Washington, DC.

The excerpt on page 80 is from *Leading Change* by John P. Kotter (Boston, MA: Harvard Business School, 1996), page 51. Copyright © 1996 by John P. Kotter.

The explanation of qualitative research on page 83 is quoted from *Beginning Qualitative Research: A Philosophic and Practical Guide* by Pamela Maykut & Richard Morehouse (Bristol, PA: The Falmer Press, 1994), page 2. Copyright © 1994 by Pamela Maykut and Richard Morehouse.

To view copyright terms and conditions for Internet materials cited here, log on to the home pages for the referenced Web sites.

During this book's preparation, all citations, facts, figures, names, addresses, telephone numbers, Internet URLs, and other pieces of information cited within were verified for accuracy. The authors and Saint Mary's Press staff have made every attempt to reference current and valid sources, but we cannot guarantee the content of any source, and we are not responsible for any changes that may have occurred since our verification. If you find an error in, or have a question or concern about, any of the information or sources listed within, please contact Saint Mary's Press.